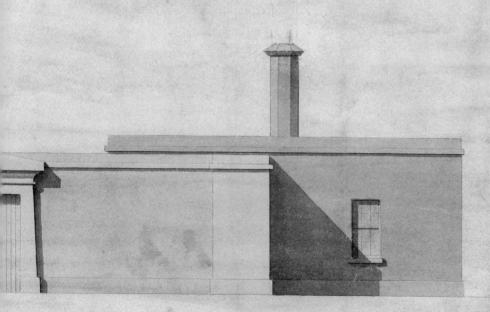

For the
Safety of All

For the Safety of All

A Story of Scotland's Lighthouses

Donald S Murray

Published in partnership between Historic Environment Scotland and the Northern Lighthouse Board

Dedicated to the men and women of the Northern Lighthouse Board, past and present

Published in 2021 by Historic Environment Scotland
Enterprises Limited SC510997

HISTORIC | ÀRAINNEACHD
ENVIRONMENT | EACHDRAIDHEIL
SCOTLAND | ALBA

Historic Environment Scotland
Longmore House
Salisbury Place
Edinburgh EH9 1SH

Historic Environment Scotland
Scottish Charity SC045925

British Library Cataloguing-in-Publication Data.
A catalogue record for this book is available from
the British Library.

ISBN 978 1 849173 10 0

Typeset in Garamond, Brunel and Gill Sans
Printed and bound in Italy by L.E.G.O. S.p.A.

MIX
Paper from
responsible sources
FSC® C023419
www.fsc.org

Front Cover

Elevation drawing for the Bell Rock lighthouse lantern by
David Alan Stevenson, dated 1 March 1900.
NLB Canmore DP088476
Gustave Doré wood engraving, originally published in the
1876 edition of *The Rime of the Ancient Mariner* by
Samuel Taylor Coleridge.
Bridgeman Images

Back Cover

Bell Rock Lighthouse, 1983, A Listed
HES Canmore SC1860225

Endpapers

Drawings showing section and north elevation of Little Ross
Island Lighthouse signed by Robert Stevenson. c1842, B Listed
NLB Canmore DP280493, DP280494

Frontispiece

Cloch Lighthouse, Inverclyde c1920, B Listed
HES Canmore SC1241842

Contents

Exile

It was the furthest inland that he'd ever been
and he missed the presence of the lighthouse beam

that had always drummed before him like a pulse,
more persistent than the tide, that stink of bladderwrack and dulse

stacked upon the shoreline near his home.
Without the radiance of that tower, he often felt alone

and longing for the cleaving of the wind, the cliff-top
on which that structure stood, where, as a child, he'd stop

and tap out imitations of the rhythms of its light —
flashing white every five seconds — into immeasurable night.

Donald S Murray

Hyskeir Lighthouse, Highland

Ian Cowe

Introduction
The Spark

Though I have only visited a comparatively small number, I feel that much of my life has been a miniature version of the tours that the Commissioners of the Northern Lighthouse Board (NLB) and others once undertook around the various lighthouses of Scotland. They sailed around the locations where these towers were positioned, circling the structures before they entered them, seeking to ensure that they were fit for the purpose for which they were designed. Probing and prodding, they would check the condition of the lighthouse's stonework and its landing place, the quality and cleanliness of the glass and the strength of the light that shone from places as far apart as Muckle Flugga and Mull of Galloway. Sniffing for dampness and decay, opening and closing the heavy wooden doors of each building, they would examine, too, the standard of accommodation on the rock, headland or island that had been provided for those who kept these lamps glowing upon the seas around the shoreline of Scotland.

My examination of lighthouses has been a shade more domestic and less dangerous than the ones

Butt of Lewis Lighthouse, Na h-Eileanan Siar A Listed
The view from the Butt – the gleam from the lighthouse once cast its glow on the crofthouses and croftland; moorland and machair, sand and shore from its stance on Rubha Robhanais, illuminating the waves of lazy beds as well as those found on the surface of the sea.
HES Canmore DP007830

undertaken by those men. It has also been done in a more distant and less judgemental fashion, almost by chance rather than design. I was brought up in Ness on the northern tip of the Isle of Lewis. Almost every hour of my young life, various guardians of the sea stood upon my cramped and narrow horizon. Along the district, to my north, there was the building we knew as the Decca Station, playing its part in charting and navigating the movement of cargo vessels and liners across the narrow channel of the Minch and the width of the North Atlantic, its giant radio transmitter circulating messages from shore to ship. Not far away was the 37 metre high red-brick tower of the Butt of Lewis lighthouse. This stood above cliffs on the edge of the island, almost – I imagined – within touching distance if I stretched out my fingers while walking down the family croft. Able to withstand storms that can reach record speeds for the British Isles, its gleam cast light on the shadows of nearby villages – such as Knockaird, Eoropie and Fivepenny – during those nights when its lamp swirled and spiralled round land as well as sea. (Nowadays, homes in the district are shielded from the intrusion of its glow, its shaft reserved for those travelling on the ocean, edging, perhaps, towards the coastline of north-west Scotland.)

Its white flash glittered on the water, catching in its sweep and circle the lights of any fishing boats anchored a short distance out from cliffs and sandy beaches of the northernmost part of Ness. Even in daytime it stayed by my side, more sacred to me than the thirteenth century Teampall Mholuaidh (St Moluag's Church) which stands only a short distance away from its tower. That chapel had been a guiding light to some of my ancestors and others in the island, who in times past would have fallen to their knees when they saw it from a hilltop where our family croft stretches down to the shore, believing it to be a place of healing, particularly for those who were plagued by issues of mental health.

Apart from the white and mustard keepers' houses, there was another structure on the headland where the lighthouse stood. Back in my childhood, before seas reared up to gnaw and swallow the cliffs which formed its foundation, a white tower guarded its side. This was the foghorn – the tallest of its kind in Scotland, designed that way because there was always the danger that breaking waves would douse and silence the strength and depth of its notes. I was alerted to its existence, however, not so much by its height but by the manner in which it sometimes shook me awake on the mornings I had to travel to Cross, my local primary school. It lowed then like a herd of village cattle having broken out of their byres, determined to make their presence heard among the local crofters. I would open the curtains on those days to see … nothing; the mist, heavy rain or snow shower that the sound of the foghorn necessitated obscuring croft and neighbours, the narrow village road, the local post office. The fact that mist blurred our vision did not put an end to the inevitable game of football that took place behind the school that day, our movements accompanied not by a referee's whistle but by the foghorn's deep bass notes. It only increased the difficulties of the goalkeeper as the ball was lashed or headed in his general direction, unable to even glimpse it before it whizzed past.

The Butt of Lewis was not the only lighthouse that featured in my childhood. Travelling east to villages like Adabrock, Skigersta or the empty settlement of Cuishader on the eastern edge of the Ness moor, I might see the light of Cape Wrath – four white flashes every thirty seconds – at the northern tip of Sutherland. It was in this abandoned location that my great-grandmother learned to pray at great volume, a characteristic which she was well-known for when she took up residence in my home village of South Dell, disturbing the neighbours with her pleas and requests. Perhaps this was to counter the loudness of the waves as they thundered below the cliffs of that high place.

Perhaps it was instead a way of seeking to convert pagan mainlanders as they settled down to eat in their homes in Durness or even distant Kinlochbervie. In our local Lewis Gaelic, the spot where the lighthouse stood at Cape Wrath was known as 'An Carbh' or the 'turning point', derived from the Old Norse *hvarf.* Its original meaning referred to the way our Viking ancestors used to turn their ships there as they sailed onwards in a variety of directions, maybe east to the Pentland Firth or southwards through the waters of the Minch, and most of my contemporaries probably thought of it in a similar way. They contemplated a time when we would stand upon a junction, wondering whether we would travel to the mainland or remain where we were, digging our foundations as deep as our local lighthouse.

Sometimes too I would hear small snatches of stories about North Rona to the north-east of Lewis, a location where a major light, erected in the mid-eighties, now stands. It would be mentioned by some of my fellow-pupils whose fathers used to gather the sheep which grazed there once a year. They would talk of the time their dads spent in that isolated island as if it was some exotic holiday they enjoyed, graced, perhaps, by some of the gannets that nested on nearby Sulasgeir hurtling downwards into the sea. 'That's where the guga comes from,' they might say, mentioning the gannet-chick that was the Nessman or Niseach's sacred, salty meal a few times every year, harvested from Sulasgeir's cliffs by a dozen men from, say, the villages at the northern tip of the district. It would be plucked and salted before arriving in our homes and kitchens, accompanied on the plate by a clutch of Kerr's Pink potatoes. 'It's great. Delicious,' they would say as they smacked their lips together, as if their fathers' journeys to the neighbouring island gave them an additional relish for its flavour.

And then I could walk along the coastline to my south towards the village of Galson. There I could try and catch a faint, half-imagined glimpse of another

Sulasgeir, Na h-Eileanan Siar
'This ile is full of wild fowls', wrote Donald Monro, the High Dean of the Isles in 1549, noting that the men of Ness went there to hunt seabirds. For all that the birds caught there may have changed – eider duck, probably, at that time and now gannets – a crew from Ness still go out to Sulasgeir today, guided by the minor light that stands there.
HES Canmore DP256787

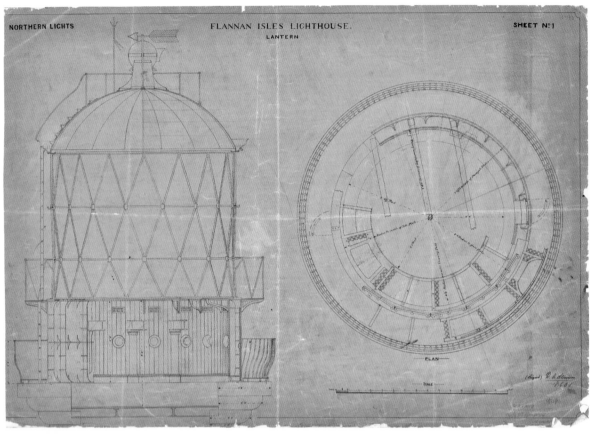

PLAN

SCALE

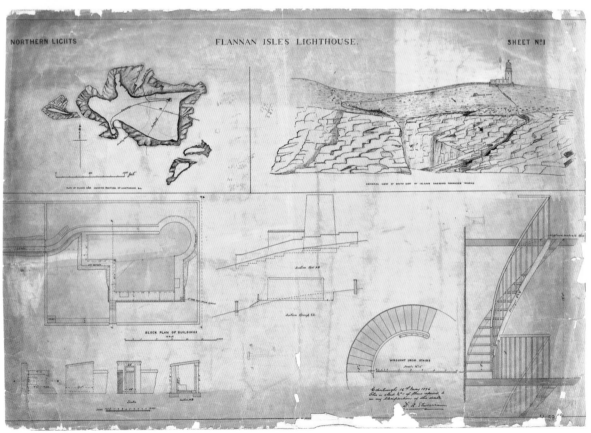

BLOCK PLAN OF BUILDINGS

WROUGHT IRON STAIRS

lighthouse, the one perched on the Flannan Isles, a building associated with a familiar tale. It was a structure that my primary school headteacher, Donald Macarthur, spoke about a great deal in his schoolroom in Cross. A native of the village of Carloway, he would sometimes break off from teaching the essential facts of arithmetic or geography to speak about the legend of this building associated with his particular edge of the world, specifically the neighbouring village of Breasclete. On one occasion he read aloud the first verse of a poem by W W Gibson that told of how:

Though three men dwell on Flannan Isle
To keep the lamp alight,
As we steered under the lee, we caught
No glimmer through the night.

It was a tale that drew us in, one that built up an eerie atmosphere by referring to three large dark birds that rested on the island's cliffs when the search-party arrived there on Boxing Day 1900 to look for the missing keepers who had failed to light the lantern for a number of consecutive nights. Gibson mentioned too the front door that lay open, the untouched meal and upturned chair that may (or may not) have been discovered by those who arrived to look for the three men – Thomas Marshall, James Ducat and Donald MacArthur – who were posted there but disappeared that winter. Our teacher, the other Donald Macarthur, noted the unexpected deaths that were associated with the lighthouse – the suicides and bouts of madness that were linked to those stationed on these islands some twenty miles west of the southern edge of Lewis, pointing out that most of this was inaccurate.

'Poetic licence,' Donald Macarthur explained to us. 'Writers are allowed to do this to increase the effect of their tale or story.'

We nodded, accepting this explanation, keeping it in store, perhaps, for the next time we were found to be guilty of telling lies by either him or our parents.

Flannan Isles Lighthouse, Na h-Eileanan Siar B Listed

Plans of the Flannan Isles lighthouse on Eilean Mòr from May 1896, showing its location, lantern and iron staircase. Clearly David Stevenson, its main architect, could not have anticipated how central this remote lighthouse would be to twentieth century (and later) storytelling.

NLB Canmore DP038542, DP005163

'We're just using poetic licence,' we might declare on these occasions. There is no doubt that the adults who have written about the Flannan Isles and the way in which the three lightkeepers disappeared from there have relied very heavily on this approach, playing fast and loose with facts. I have read, for instance, that there were – allegedly – references to the state of mind of the keepers in the pages of the official journal they kept, that Marshall noted that the officer in command, Ducat, was 'irritable' during the sea-storm that lashed the island during mid-December, and that the third individual MacArthur was 'crying' like a child throughout the ocean's uproar. Even sea-monsters and dragons have risen from the depths to snatch away the custodians of the light, dragging their victims into caverns below the waves. Aliens have come from the opposite direction, swooping downwards to abduct the keepers. Doctor Who – in his Tom Baker incarnation – has even landed on an island in his Tardis where a similar incident occurred. The story of the Flannan Isles is mysteriously transported to the English coast in the episode called 'The Horror of Fang Rock', which contained the immortal line that lightkeepers might have employed in certain situations, with Doctor Who explaining how he arrived there with the words: 'the localised conditions of planetary atmospheric condensation caused a malfunction in the visual orientation circuits. Or to put it another way, we got lost in the fog.'

And then there are the other ways the story has been transformed. Peter Maxwell Davies shaped it into an opera, *The Lighthouse*. A film *The Vanishing* starring Gerard Butler and Peter Mullen rolled out in 2019. The British rock group Genesis recorded a song based on the tale. All of this has in some way stemmed from Gibson's original use of 'poetic licence', embellishing what was – when it was first recorded by the authorities – a simple, coherent story, easily explained. As John Love informs us in his book *A Natural History of Lighthouses*, two of the men had previously been fined for failing to store away a rope and a crane properly. It was to check that both this and other tasks had been done that two of the men had stepped out of the lighthouse door towards the landing slip, only to be washed away by the turbulence and strength of the seas that day. The other may have followed them outdoors – either to warn them of an incoming wave or to look for them after they had vanished from the building for a while. Whatever the

Bressay Lighthouse, Shetland c1870 B Listed

At one time David Stevenson argued that building a lighthouse in
the waters around Shetland would be impossible, too dangerous
and expensive. Bressay lighthouse, built in 1858 opposite the east
coast of the mainland of Shetland, is proof that this argument
did not hold sway. It still stands guard over the 'sooth mooth' or
southern entrance to Lerwick harbour today.

HES Canmore DP073865

reason, he experienced a similar fate, his body swept up by the oceans like his companions. And as a result of all this, for the next few nights, the 'blinded lantern', to use the words of Gibson, 'never shot a spark / Of comfort through the dark'.

There have been other lighthouses in my life since. They have included Skerryvore, which sheds its light on the waters around Tiree, the ancestral home of one set of my grandparents, and the structures, too, in Bressay in Shetland and the Monach Isles off the coast of Benbecula and its neighbours in the Western Isles. When nights are still and clear, the glow of the last two can be seen twinkling through the windows of houses where I lived or still live, almost like a pulse beating through either the sitting room or kitchen. I may not have the close acquaintance that the various justices, provosts and other luminaries experienced in the past, visiting lighthouses on their annual 'adventure' round these islands, but there has been a closeness and steadiness to our relationship, as if, for much of my life, they have kept pace and in close contact with me.

And so this book is not principally a work of history nor a detailed, scientific account of how lighthouses operate or were built.

In part, it is a reminder of those members of the Stevenson family who did so much to ensure the construction of these towers on islands, peninsulas and the coastline's edge in both Scotland and the Isle of Man – many of which still stand today, around 150 as listed buildings. These are structures listed by Historic Environment Scotland for their special and historical importance and are categorised as A, B or C according to their standing and significance. These listed buildings demonstrate Scotland's character, illustrating both the nation's unique sense of place and the wealth of its heritage. They include the work of founder of the engineering dynasty, Robert Stevenson, who built the Bell Rock lighthouse among others; his eldest son Alan, whose creations included Skerryvore lighthouse; his younger brothers David and Thomas, who built over 30 lighthouses in their time; and, in the early years of the twentieth century, the next generation, Charles and David Alan, who continued the work of the family around the Scottish coast. Their constant and distinctive patterns reinforced the purpose of the lighthouses. It is one summed up by the motto of the Northern Lighthouse Board, the organisation that since its inception in 1786 has done so much to help create and maintain them, continuing the tradition of innovation in lighthouse engineering and technology. They exist *In Salutem Omnium* – for the safety of all.

But mainly this book is a love-letter to lighthouses, a paean of praise to their fidelity and continual presence in my life.

Let them shine.

Chapter 1
The Absence of Illumination
The Earliest Lighthouses

'S tu fialaidh glic do chiall gun tig,
Air dìomhaireachd nan reultan

Uilleam MacCoinnich (Loch Carrann)
'Òran do nighean Fear na Comraich'

And you generous, wise,
your reason shall illuminate
the mystery of the stars

William MacKenzie (Lochcarron)
'Song to the Daughter of the Applecross Man'

Frequently, during my childhood and teenage years, there were reminders of the depth of darkness that existed for centuries around the coastline of this country.

At night or early evening, a storm might rattle windows, a gust of wind puff above chimney tops. The lights across the house would falter and flicker before disappearing. After that, there would be a scramble for matches and candles, a torch if there was one to be found. A Tilley lamp would be lit, taking a moment or two to ignite and burn before its warm glow added intricacies of light and shade to a room which seconds earlier had been illuminated only by the flame of a peat fire. It was as if we had stepped back in history, into the period before electricity had come to our homes, the ages swirling into reverse for a moment or two.

And that change was most apparent when we peered out of the window at the rest of the village and the broad stretch of the moor. Apart from the spin and eddy of the Butt of Lewis lighthouse, the stillness of the red light above the Decca Station and the rare sweep of a set of car headlights, all was in darkness. We could imagine the householders performing the same rituals we did – scuttling through the kitchen cabinet or chest of drawers for matches, looking in the understairs cupboard among sheets and blankets for the lamp – before they restored muted light to their homes. This was what might have been seen in these houses if a passer-by had peeked in. The faint glimmer of firelight. The subdued flame of a Tilley lamp. Or perhaps even more dim and pale than any of these lanterns – a wick dipped in the oil of a seabird, seal or whale. An unsteady flicker casting more shade than light into the room.

The scale of this darkness was one of the factors that made travel around the British Isles difficult for centuries. Difficult enough on land, this was

Pharos of Alexandria, Egypt

In 1968, the ruins of this ancient lighthouse were rediscovered by a team of marine archaeologists. In 1994, these were investigated further, underwater photographers recording the remains of scattered columns and statues. Since then, satellite imaging has revealed more and it is now possible to go diving among ruins destroyed many centuries ago by a succession of earthquakes.

Nineteenth century illustration – Private Collection/Bridgeman Images

especially the case when boats were the main mode of transport. Until the expansion of road and rail, after all, the seas and waterways were Scotland's main highways. The seasons intensified travel problems, especially during late autumn and winter. In many ways, the sailors and travellers of these early times lived the opposite kind of lives to the modern city dweller. The latter's constant use of electric light, whether found in the streets they walk and drive through or within their homes, prevents them seeing the moon and stars above their heads. For those who made journeys either on shore or at sea in the past, there were sometimes contrary issues. The need to observe and navigate by the stars made them focus overhead, leading – occasionally – to failure to see the rocks and skerries that loomed out of the ocean, the unpredictable nature of both depths and shoreline.

And then there was the unreliable character of light before the arrival of the lighthouse to these shores, a process that began in earnest around the commencement of the nineteenth century. Sometimes, when a storm buffeted their boat, the glow of fire on the coastline meant safety and security for sailors, a harbour where a vessel could be tied up and fastened until that night's tempest passed. However, there were occasions when their need for shelter and protection made mariners too easily deceived. Allegedly wreckers on the coastline of these islands took advantage of their desperation, ushering them to a shore where the consignment of goods aboard would be plundered, their lives lost. Fires would be lit, and signals flashed, but their boats were ushered only in the direction of danger. Over the course of the nineteenth century and later, the Stevenson family and the Northern Lighthouse Board put an end to these practices. Their lighthouses were charted and mapped. If anything flickered elsewhere, as it sometimes had in the past, it would most likely be a trick or a ruse, a deadly trap.

There were other hazards in the northern edge of the world in summer. During this season, those of us who live in places like the north of Scotland have the sun as an almost constant companion. Its presence, in some shape or form, rarely leaves the sky, creating a continual twilight, blurring at most to a shade of ochre in the sky. The persistent lack of rhythm of light and dark has its effect on people, making some edgy and ill-at-ease. Insomnia abounds: attention wanders. Storm-clouds and dangers on the horizon

can fail to be seen. Mist, particularly on Scotland's east coast, prone to haar, can obscure and conceal the risks ahead.

It was this – their awareness of the constant threat of terrors posed by both human actions and seaborne life – that made men begin to build lighthouses, a way of making the existence of both ship and crew more secure and safe. It was a process that began back around 280 BC on the north coast of Africa, where the Pharos of Alexandria was built. Though some facts about the structure are disputed, this grandiose building, decorated with sphinx and statues, stood some 100m high; the range of its light – whether an open fire or a lantern, no one is quite certain – boosted by a curved mirror. The structure lasted for around fifteen centuries, until it crumbled in the aftermath of two earthquakes in 1303 and 1323. Its influence persisted for even longer: it is found in the term 'pharology', the study of lighthouses, as well as in the name for at least ten of the Northern Lighthouse Board's own vessels. The first *Pharos* came into service in 1807 as a support vessel when the Bell Rock light was being built; the latest of that name came into service in 2007, precisely two centuries later.

The original Pharos, the glory of Egypt's ancient leaders, the Ptolemies, was a structure known in legend as one of the Seven Wonders of the World (together with the Hanging Garden of Babylon, the Great Pyramid of Giza, the Colossus of Rhodes,[1] the Statue of Zeus at Olympia, the Temple of Artemis at Ephesus, and the Mausoleum at Halicarnassus). Some centuries later, other lighthouses were built – many in stone – witness to the might of the later Roman Empire. There was one in Portus erected by the Emperor Claudius, who governed the Empire from AD41 to 54. Its light was said by Pliny the Younger to offer the prospect of saving 'countless lives by providing a haven on this long stretch of harbourless coast', guiding ships near the Italian coastline north of Ostia, the harbour city of Ancient Rome. No more than a quarter of the size of its Egyptian predecessor, nothing of it now survives, apart from a few underwater remains uncovered by archaeologists in the twenty-first century. In this, it is not dissimilar to other lighthouses built by the Romans, many of which now lie forgotten or in ruins.

1 There is, too, the view that the Colossus of Rhodes – built in 3000 BC – also acted as a lighthouse, guiding ships to harbour by its light.

Tower of Hercules, A Coruña, Spain

PHAS/UIG / Bridgeman Images

There are exceptions, such as the Tower of Hercules light that still stands outside the town of A Coruña in Galicia in the north-west corner of Spain. This is said to have been constructed in the early second century during the reign of Emperor Trajan, the soldier-emperor who ruled from AD 98 to 117. Largely renovated in 1791, its lamp still glimmers over the area the Romans believed to be the 'end of the earth', the expression providing the name Finisterra for the region. The lamp's necessity is underlined by one of its other names, Costa da Morte ('Coast of Death'),

a nickname given to the area by the sheer number of shipwrecks that occurred there. There are also the remains of another Roman lighthouse, built around AD 50, found within the walls of Dover Castle on the southern coast of England, its fiery glow once clearly marking a safe route across the English Channel.

There were other kings and emperors – such as the Frankish ruler Charlemagne in the ninth century – who attempted to revive the lighthouse building traditions of Egypt and Rome. There was one near Boulogne on the coast of northern France which stood till the cliff on which it had been constructed collapsed into the sea in 1644. Sometimes their efforts were more temporary than that. The French King Louis IX

Kõpu Lighthouse, Hiiumaa Island, Estonia

Dmitry Malov / Alamy Stock Photo

Cordouan Tower, Gironde Estuary, France

Adafim / Alamy Stock Photo

Hook Head Lighthouse, Co. Wexford, Ireland

Stephen Emerson / Alamy Stock Photo

Europa Point Lighthouse, Gibraltar

incamerastock / Alamy Stock Photo

was said to have placed a lantern on the Tour de Constance at Aigues-Mortes in southern France when his ships sailed from their home harbours to fight in the Crusades in the middle of the thirteenth century.

It was not, however, the whims and will of rulers that gave rise to the number of lighthouses that are found around European coastlines even today. They partly came into existence because of the demands and requirements of maritime trade. One – the Lanterna – was built to guide ships into the port of Genoa during the twelfth century. Rebuilt in 1543, the tower reached an impressive 76 metres – or 117 metres if one included the rock that formed its base. This example was followed by the merchants of the German Hanseatic League, who built lighthouses around much of the Baltic from the early thirteenth century onwards. Some of these were rudimentary – braziers lifted high on poles. Others, like the Kõpu lighthouse on Hiiumaa in Estonia, were more substantial. Finally completed by 1531, a bonfire was lit upon its stone tower. Another area which possessed a substantial number was the coastline of Flanders, largely to assist the ships involved in the cloth trade. One of their fire-towers in Nieuwpoort, built in 1284, stood until the First World War, when it was blown up during the fighting. The Cordouan tower near Bordeaux at the mouth of the Gironde estuary in France has also enjoyed a long existence. Completed in 1611, it still stands today.

There was also the occasional monastery that maintained fires to alert sailors to the dangers around the peninsulas and islands their buildings occupied. One of the most remarkable is Hook Head, east of Waterford Harbour, in County Wexford, Ireland. Peculiarly, I first heard about this in the vicinity of Europa Point lighthouse in Gibraltar. There was much that was exotic and strange about that location – the prevailing heat, the large mosque standing nearby, that sense of being at the centre of the world and not as usual at its edge – but also a little that was familiar, the lighthouse tower with its red and white band, the similarity of the Moroccan coastline across the sea to the mountains of Sutherland I had observed so often in my youth and – most especially – the wind that gusted across that edge of land. The Irish dancer Aine Stapleton was part of the group who had travelled to Gibraltar to take part in

the NatWest International Island Games, a four-yearly sporting event involving many of the world's island communities. She said that, like me, she was reminded of home, especially the lighthouse at Hook Head, one of the oldest in the world and a source of inspiration for her.

Later I checked up on it – how the existing tower had been there since the twelfth century, how the first guardians of the light were a group of monks whose monastery stood on the peninsula. They lit warning fires to inform sailors of the treacherous rocks that studded the area, highlighting the dangers that lay around. In this, they were probably not unusual. The women living on the shoreline of certain locations must have frequently lit bonfires to ensure their men were safe when they took to sea in coracle or boat. The monks based on the Monach Isles, in the lee of Benbecula and North Uist, performed similar duties to their counterparts in Wexford, alerting those at sea to the presence of perils nearby. One can even imagine the holy man who might have occupied the sixth century chapel that still stands on the Flannan Isles today (and features in Neil Gunn's novel *The Silver Darlings*) setting off a similar blaze when a rare vessel intruded into that particular stretch of the Atlantic during his time within that tiny, cramped building.

And the same steps were taken by the monks of the Benedictine order on the Isle of May in the north of the Firth of Forth, attempting to prevent the frequent loss of both lives and boats nearby. They might guide pilgrims, too, to their shores, where they placed stones on a cairn to St Ethernan or Adrian, who may have died there during Viking raids in AD 875. The cairns pointed to the holy shrines of St Andrews, ensuring that no one became lost on that particular route to grace.

There were other measures elsewhere. Beacons marking the entrances to both Leith and Aberdeen harbours are noted to have been in existence in around 1553 and 1566. There are records too of lights, maintained by clerics, at Portpatrick and, possibly, Fair Isle. Lights probably shone in certain windows, such as one in Dunyvaig Castle on the island of Islay. Various church towers – like those in Crail Parish Church in north-east Fife – are noted as being landmarks for sailors nearing those ports. Sometimes, there may just have been stone markers without benefit of lights – a cairn, a pillar, a waymark that showed people they were in the right direction for home.[2]

But for much of the coastline, for centuries, there was darkness. This was especially true of the west coast of Scotland which unlike, say, Leith, Dundee or Aberdeen, was far away from the trade that grew up across the North Sea, where merchants exchanged goods like salt fish, hides, wool, and – later – wheat, rye and malt, for the likes of flax, fine cloth and wine. Stone markers were generally used on the dark western edge. Wood, on the rare occasions it was ever washed ashore on the treeless islands of, say, the Hebrides, Orkney or Shetland, was certainly not to be wasted as fuel for flame and heat. There were other, infinitely more practical ways in which it could be employed.

In 1636, about the same time as King Charles I authorised the building of a series of beacons around the coastline of Ireland, including the Old Head of Kinsale, Scotland finally obtained its first 'lighthouse' by order of the king. It stood on the Isle of May – where monks had once fired the flames of their own version of a hazard light. A three-storey tower 7.5m square and 12m high, this structure took advantage of the island's position near the Forth coalfields by having a coal-fired flame on its roof, the fuel heaved and hauled in pans via a rope-and-pulley to the brazier on the summit. For all that this was more effective than wood in terms of the quality of light, more compact and requiring less care when it rained, there were major disadvantages. For example, it consumed some 200 tons of coal every year. On a wild, wintry night, as much as three tons could be burnt. In high winds or mist, it produced – to coin a phrase – a great deal more smoke than light, sometimes obscuring landfall with its dark shadow. At other times, all the keeper's art and craft would be needed to prevent it burning on one side only, fanned by the prevailing winds. There was also the possibility that mariners could confuse the light produced by coal with those produced by industry or houses.

A coal-fired light also meant an uncomfortable existence for the lightkeeper who had – on occasion

Isle of May Lighthouse and The Beacon, Former Lighthouse Building, Fife B Listed / Scheduled

Clearly the principal Scottish lighthouse of the seventeenth century, the original building was a three-storey tower with a square plan. When Robert Stevenson built the replacement light in 1816 it was obscured by the old lighthouse. Following the intervention of Sir Walter Scott, Stevenson truncated the structure, rather than demolishing it. In 2017, a group of architects and engineers worked with NLB and HES to ensure its survival for many years to come.

Ian Cowe / HES Canmore DP210897

– to carry the coal from the shoreline on his back. There were other difficult conditions endured by both him and his family, as they had to live below the light – all this for the very small reward of £7 per year in 1786. It was a situation that ended in tragedy on one occasion in the Isle of May. In January 1791, the keeper George Anderson, his wife and five of their children were killed, suffocated by the fumes from the partly burnt ashes that were piled a short distance from their residence. One child, Lucy – a baby at the time – survived, going on to marry one of the men, Henry Dowie, 22 years her senior, who had rescued her. Two of the assistant lightkeepers were also affected, rendered unconscious by the smoke but recovering later. The original lighthouse was privately owned but the NLB took over responsibility when the current light was built in 1815.

It was not the only light in Scotland by this time. In 1687 there were, for instance, two leading lights built on Buddon Ness near Carnoustie at the mouth of the River Tay. As noted by historian David Worthington, there were a number in place for the Firthland ferries. When people sought to cross the Moray, Dornoch or Cromarty Firth, their vessels were summoned by 'blazes' lit by their potential passengers, guiding them to shore. (The same happened at North Queensferry, where a signal house was positioned.) These were certainly in place in Nigg, Meikle Ferry and Chanonry Point. Existing till the early years of the nineteenth century, these voyages of little more than a mile between passenger collection points shortened considerably the journeys of those travelling between various parts of Scotland's meandering north-eastern coast. They were also considerably safer than the open sea.

There was an early lighthouse on the west coast too, erected near Portpatrick around 1680. This

2 My own view is that there would have been many more of these markers. There were monks on many islands around the Scottish coast. It has been suggested that the Vikings would have put beacons in place, allowing their vessels to travel south to Dublin. One of the clan-crests of the Macleods of Lewis bears a blaze which underlines the possibility. It has also been theorised that brochs were used to aid the progress of ships round the coast.

was a precursor of change to come, the balance of the country altering and shifting. The Act of Union of 1707 meant that the west coast of Scotland could begin to trade with the continent of America, including the West Indies, across the wide stretch of the Atlantic, with money being made from sugar, tobacco, cotton – and enslaved people. Initially it was Dumfries that benefited, an important port at that time with connections to Liverpool and Ireland. A beacon was commissioned at Southerness on the Solway Firth in 1748, which became a lighthouse by 1811. It is still upright today, one of the oldest in the country for all that it was decommissioned in 1936 and was never the responsibility of the Northern Lighthouse Board.

A few years later, however, the balance continued to shift. The trading merchants, initially of the town of Irvine, but later Port Glasgow and finally Glasgow itself, established the first statutory lighthouse authority, the Trustees of the Clyde Lights, in 1756. It was different in many ways to its predecessors, especially in the manner it was funded. Dues were paid to trustees, who used the money only for the upkeep and maintenance of lights – not for the profit of private individuals as had happened on the Isle of May, or a collective of sailors, for instance, in Dundee. A year later, the trustees erected a building that was not dissimilar to the one on the Isle of May, a tower with an open fire on its crest, on Little Cumbrae in the Firth of Clyde. It suffered from all the problems of its predecessor: smoke billowing from its summit and obscuring the view; the sheer weight and quantity of fuel required. But in its own way it heralded change – not only in the way it was financed but also in terms of its position in the geography of Scotland.

Yet, for all that, there were still only a handful of lighthouses in the country by 1760. They were all relatively rudimentary and ill-suited for the purpose for which they were made, sparks in the darkness rather than the bright gleams that were needed.

Southerness Lighthouse, Dumfries & Galloway A Listed

A particularly fine example of an eighteenth century lighthouse, Southerness lighthouse acts as a reminder that there was a time when roads in the south-west of Scotland were poor and most travel and transport occurred by sea.

HES 008-000-013-065-R

Chapter 2
A Cone of Light
Kinnaird Head and the Museum of Scottish Lighthouses

All quiet, all dark: excepting where
A cone of light stood on the pier

Norman MacCaig, 'Midnight, Lochinver'

One of the great pleasures in visiting the Museum of Scottish Lighthouses in Fraserburgh is that it enables a visitor to look at lighthouses through a different kind of lens. It did this – for me – even before I walked through its rounded entrance, partly because of the geographical situation the building lies in. Wrapped up in scarf and gloves, I spent some time strolling the streets of this north-east fishing port, listening to the different music of the voices I overheard. It was not a sound overfamiliar to me. The majority spoke Doric, talking to each other about the chill edge of the wind, how the weather had turned wintry, asking about each other's welfare.

'Fit like? Far hiv ye bin?'

I walked around, as per my usual practice, noting the ships that were tied up, many avoiding the force

of the gale, the stomach-stirring swell of the sea, that was in evidence that day. Among the Fraserburgh boats with names like *Deep Harmony IV*, *Bountiful* and *Shamariah*, I noticed a red-sided fishing vessel with the registration 'CY 250' – the *Stella Maris* from Castlebay in the isle of Barra. I abandoned my sense of being alone. My fellow Gaels had been here before – just as I recalled the Buckie, Peterhead and Fraserburgh boats being tied up in the Stornoway of my youth, the crews' accents odd and different among the Gaelic speakers of districts like my native Ness or Tolsta, or even the fishermen of Stornoway whose distinctive vowels stretched out and extended like the fishing nets that lay sprawled along the quayside.

'H-o-w-'s i-t g-o-i-n-g, c-o-v-e?'

That sense of Fraserburgh or the 'Broch' being an alien place was lessened still further when I stepped into the museum, an adapted fish-store with a sloping floor and an extended roof. Behind it stood Kinnaird Head Lighthouse and the lightkeepers' dwellings with their mustard and white walls, shades familiar to me from my youth. Even the name 'Kinnaird Head' was originally Gaelic – 'An Ceann Àrd' or the 'High Headland'. And then there were the friendly faces of the staff – Michael Cruickshank behind the counter of the museum as he handed out the ticket and brochure.

'The tour of the lighthouse will begin at 11am. You can wander round the museum until then.' I nodded, resisting the temptation to settle down on a peculiar glass-backed sofa which had once been on the deck of

Kinnaird Head Lighthouse, Aberdeenshire A Listed

Of all the lighthouses in Scotland, Kinnaird Head in Fraserburgh has undergone the most transformations. Part of it was once Kinnaird Head Castle, a building begun initially by Sir Alexander Fraser, the 8th Laird of Philorth, in 1570. Its metamorphosis continued in 1787 when it was leased to the trustees of the Northern Lights, who turned it into a lighthouse …

Ian Cowe

the *Pharos*, one of three ships owned by the Northern Lighthouse Board to service the NLB lights and to transport the Commissioners around the country's periphery on their inspection voyages. Instead, I went past this in the direction of six identical circular lenses lined up behind it, part of the Rhinns of Islay lighthouse until they were removed in 1978. At one time, the entire optic to which they belonged was a larger structure, forming a cage of glass. But these six 'bullseyes', as they were known, are all that now remain in existence, creating both a wall and a rather opaque window for the remainder of the museum. Stretched out above this are the names of lighthouses, scrolled on white panels and ringing like the chorus of a song that might have been boomed out in an old Highland ceilidh 50 years ago, the feet of the audience stamping the rhythm of the words.

'N Unst', 'Butt of Lewis', 'Girdle Ness', 'Lochindaal', …

The signs ripple to a close with words like 'Sanda', 'Monach', 'Flannan Isles', all names that summon up ghosts and vacancies, places which have either lost their human population or where – in the case of Sanda – the number of people has dwindled to a few.

It is this sense of emptiness that is underlined by the next room the visitor enters. There is something spectral about the lights that are gathered there, the ghosts of lighthouse lenses past casting their glow in a windowless room filled with shadows. It's as if Doctor Who's Tardis has come to rest here, but without the whirl of wind noises that used to accompany its touchdown, though in reality that particular sound must have circled around them often enough. A fourth wall is breached – the one between past and present – and we are back in the days when the men from the Northern Lighthouse Board used to scurry up and down steps to care for the lamps which men on board nearby vessels depended on for their safety.

The names of the places where they once beamed and shone accompany me as I walk. There's Fair Isle South (the last manned light) with its unusual light – four white flashes every 40 seconds – which was first installed in the lighthouse there in 1892. A stationary lens at its centre is surrounded by vertical prisms, which look almost like household blinds. These apparently rotated round the lens, directing the light. There's Neist Point lighthouse in Skye – a 3 tonne lens cooped within a cage. It flashed twice every 30 seconds and also floated and turned through the use of a large

mercury bath or trough instead of the steel rollers that were otherwise often employed. (There were both advantages and drawbacks to this. The positive side to the change was that the light could be pushed around with one finger. The negative side was that the mercury had its own trials and tribulations. If tiny pieces of grit flecked and sullied the bath, the lens would shudder, its rotation lost. This meant that it had to be regularly emptied and cleaned.)

The model from Turnberry lighthouse is also distinctive and different. Its glass lenses were removed in the 1950s, substituted by parabolic – or curved – mirror reflectors. Less expensive than lenses, these were developed by Charles Stevenson who, while never officially an engineer to the Northern Lighthouse Board, worked with his brother David Alan Stevenson on many inventions. The entire apparatus – which looks like a metal-framed prototype for the scanning devices seen at airport security – had to complete its rotation every 36 seconds, each mirror creating its own flash. There are others, too, alongside various smaller lanterns and buoys, that are equally unusual: Corran Point, which had red glass screens where the light was magnified by the lens, pointing it in a specific direction; Dunnet Head from the north of Caithness; Chanonry Point in the Black Isle; Hoxa Head in Orkney…

And then there is my own exercise in time travel. Among the exhibits stored within the museum is one I recalled standing beside some 50 years ago as I looked across Ness in the company of lightkeeper Donald John Smith, who was known in the locality as the Bodach Dubh. This was the set of lenses of the Butt of Lewis lighthouse. Installed back in 1905, its light had circled our district through these lenses for 80 years before it was removed in 1985. Since then, it had been one of three offered to the National Maritime Museum in London, though, thankfully, another had been selected. After that, it was proposed to send the lenses to Eilean Glas lighthouse as its new owners planned to exhibit it there, before perceiving a certain

Museum of Scottish Lighthouses
Today Kinnaird Head lighthouse casts its beam occasionally, part of the buildings that make up the Museum of Scottish Lighthouses in Fraserburgh. It is now one of a series of structures that shed light both on the history and present-day situation of lighthouses within this country.
HES Canmore DP137567

difficulty with its size and scale. The next option was the local historical centre, Comunn Eachdraidh Nis, who wanted it for their premises. The set of lenses lay for many years outside the old Lionel School in the district, before it was again concluded that it was too large. After that, it was claimed by the Museum of Scottish Lighthouses in 1996, some eleven years after it had been removed. It only finally became part of one of the largest collections of lenses in the world in 2017, enabling me to recall the day 50 years earlier I gained a new and startling perspective on my local parish, its rocks and moorland, crofts and churches, seeing it from above and not – as I normally did – straining my neck to look at my home district from down below.

There were other journeys I undertook in Fraserburgh that day, mostly in the company of three of the museum employees, Lynda McGuigan the Museum Manager, Michael Strachan the Collections Manager and an important lighthouse historian, and Michael Cruickshank the Retail Manager. They all seemed to me to provide different ways of tracking the world of the lighthouse, offering their own talents and outlooks. From Glasgow, Lynda is a passionate advocate for both the museum and Fraserburgh as a whole. Chair of the local tourist board, she showed me a short film that displayed the area's attractions – locations such as Sandhaven Harbour, Troup Head and Rattray Head lighthouse – while I was in her office. Her curiosity was, however, wider than this, telling me she had studied Gaelic at university and was currently working on a PhD on Pictish stones. 'The last's one of my two great passions,' she grinned. 'The other one's museums.'

At one point she said, 'You've got to think of the good of people when you put together a place like this. If you're not going to use this for their benefit, you might as well put all of this in a store somewhere.' Underlining this, she revealed her pride in the fact that the building in her charge is an autism friendly museum.

A short time later, she left me in the care of Michael Strachan, who deciphered a great deal about all I saw there. With the museum guidebook in my hand, he helped introduce me to the terminology of lenses, one that possessed a vocabulary of its own. He mentioned bullseyes, pointing out that a lone lens produced a single flash while two or more together created a group flash. There were also, for instance, lower, central and upper reflective panels, the central one being the lens

axis, directly shining outwards from the focal point. The largest size of lens was called a hyper-radial, with a focal distance of 1330mm. The small lens used in major lighthouses tended to be the fourth order. This was 250mm and could be seen up to 12 or so miles away.[1]

It became evident that many of the lens makers were French, especially the nineteenth century ones. 'Chanonry Point, 1846 – Letourneau, Paris … Ailsa Craig, 1886 – Barbier and Fenestre, Paris … Ardnamurchan, 1849 – Letourneau, Paris … Rhinns of Islay, 1896 – Barbier and Bernard, Paris …'

It is only in the early twentieth century that the names of English firms – such as Chance Brothers, Birmingham – begin to predominate. Clearly, they had come late to the market, the French possessing an advantage in the early years of the Northern Lighthouse Board and the work of the Stevenson family, although after 1851 there was increasing use of Chance lenses, beginning with the leading lights at the River Tay.

Michael spoke about the different fuels that were used to keep the lighthouse beams lit. These ranged from fish, whale and sperm oil (the last two very important to Scotland's economy throughout the years when whalers used to arrive in ports like nearby Peterhead or Dundee) to various forms of vegetable oil, including one derived from rapeseed, called colza, which was used in many lighthouses, and later still, paraffin. And then there were the ways in which the museum sought to convey the lightkeepers' view of the world, how they composed songs to mark their lifestyle, carved out dolls houses and fashioned clocks in their spare time, augmenting their small incomes by selling the work of their hands.

We also spent time talking about the collections of photographs in the museum's possession. These include the Allardyce Collection from the 1980s and 1990s, which Anna Watt, who works in the museum office, had gone through assiduously and carefully. These showed lightkeepers at both work and leisure: one of the Fair Isle men, for instance, posing with a fiddle tucked under his chin. We also spoke about the early twentieth century photographs taken of many of Scotland's lighthouses between 1905 and 1913 by C Dick Peddie, who was then Secretary of the Northern Lighthouse Board. He captured 3D images

1 see https://uslhs.org/hyper-radial-lenses

Stewart Thomson, Fair Isle Lighthouse Keeper, c1985

Allardyce Collection, Museum of Scottish Lighthouses

of his companions on the annual lighthouse inspection voyages, using the stereoscopic method that was popular at that time – bringing two pictures together in a camera that had two separate lenses. They would then be looked at through a viewer that brought the pair of images together with both clarity and depth.

Some of Peddie's photos are technical, showing the lens found within a particular lighthouse. Others show a specific situation – how materials were loaded onto a tramway destined for Muckle Flugga in Unst, the approach to Pentland Skerries lighthouse, the Bressay foghorn engine, air-tanks being delivered at Langness in the Isle of Man. Others still are dramatic or scenic – the *Pharos* pitching in a narrow channel, a small boat full of the Commissioners making their way to Skerryvore, the construction of the tower at Rubha Reidh, the North Carr light vessel, the ancient chapel on the Flannan Isles.

There are others in the Peddie collection which are considerably less formal – snapshots of dignitaries like the Sheriff Principal of Dumfries and Galloway, Lord Darling or the Provost of Aberdeen caught in all their splendour as they indulge in some of the activities that took place on either the *Hesperus* or the *Pharos*. They clamber down lighthouse steps, their backsides jutting out above the water's edge; play the game of shuffleboard on the boat-deck; coax and persuade a mule to abandon its usual stubbornness and make its way across the isle of Pladda alongside Arran; hover dangerously as they are winched up by a landing platform, stepping up on a narrow, circular 'button' before their feet are brought to land on Skerryvore, the Pentland Skerries or the Butt of Lewis. Most of all, however, Peddie, who was an excellent caricaturist and artist, captures these figures asleep: Baillie Inches in his full multi-dimensional slumber; Baillie Inches snoozing in a deck chair. One can almost sense the snores loud and clear above the engine sounds of the vessel.

'Who's Jim?' I ask, spotting this individual working a pulley, enjoying a pipeful of tobacco, addressing a mule. 'We think that's Peddie's brother,' Michael laughs. 'He's in quite a few of them.'

I must confess to taking a great deal of pleasure in this journey through history, drawing the wooden handle of the stereoscopic viewer back and forth, blurring the images, a few moments later making them sharp again. Peddie's photographs draw us into the past, reminding us that even figures of authority at the turn of the previous century had their off-guard moments, times in which they could allow their upper lips to loosen and relax. We see them in their full humanity and not simply in the roles that they acted at that time.

Yet even this is not as thorough an experience as the one Michael Cruickshank had in store for me. It is his task to take me out to visit the museum's neighbour, Kinnaird Head lighthouse – surely one of the most unusual structures of its kind in the country. It not only served as a light for the many vessels that sailed or steamed this way, but was also the remaining tower of Fraserburgh Castle, constructed in 1571 by Sir Alexander Fraser, 8th Laird of Philorth. The headland on which it was built was also the basis for other dreams and ambitions, including a plan to build a university nearby. Little remains. Even the tower only exists because of the work that was done when it was transformed into the first light that the newly

C Dick Peddie Collection

A game of shuffleboard, clambering up a ladder, being suspended between boat and shore – just some of activities recorded by C Dick Peddie, the Edinburgh-born secretary of the Northern Lighthouse Board, during the annual visits of the Commissioners to various lighthouses around the Scottish coastline between 1905 and 1913. These striking images reveal much of what they encountered on their inspections.

Peddie Collection, Museum of Scottish Lighthouses

formed Northern Lighthouse Board brought into existence in 1787.

The wind whips against us as we step out of the door, transforming the sea into white jagged crests; each surge accompanied by a flurry and spit of rain. We cower as we walk past a white-walled smokehouse, now unused, and the building that they call the Wine Tower, a mysterious three-storey stone structure which is also believed to have been built around 1570. It stands in contrast to a more modern construction, the new automatic light that is dwarfed by the stone of its distinctive predecessor. Built in 1991, it has little of either the scale or the eccentricity of the lighthouse that was employed for centuries before. However, this replacement is both dependable and reliable, the major priorities of our modern ages. If the main optic fails, there are two emergency LEDs on either side of the lantern. This light, unlike the original, is never likely to be entirely doused.

There are other buildings too – those where the lightkeepers dwelt, not unlike the ones that stand alongside the Butt of Lewis lighthouse. Alongside is the building occupied by an array of Kelvin-diesel engines, pristine and sparkling, for all that they have been in place since 1950. These drive the air-compressors, the means by which the low-pitched sound of the nearby foghorn was created, powered by a weight and air-driven clockwork mechanism. The sound of every lighthouse foghorn was distinct and different, each one designed to be heard 10 miles away. I glance at this as I go past, heading for our destination.

Michael pushes open the heavy door of the lighthouse, revealing the stairs within. The red and cream steps swirl round and round the building, reminding me of the sheer circularity of a lightkeeper's life. The lamp's revolution as it shines upon the waters of the North Sea. The wheeling of seabirds to and from the coasts where their nests are built. Gulls, kittiwakes, even starlings. The days of leave when a man from a remote station might be with his family followed by these times when – just as I do in the trail of Michael's footsteps – they spend much of their time clambering upwards to the light. Life as a continual whirl, a constant circuit. It is all the stranger to find this within the box-like shape of this lighthouse.

On this occasion, I stop on the way, something that the lightkeepers might have done before they climbed onwards to go into the Hall. The name is a reminder that this was at one point the principal room of the original castle, where Sir Alexander Fraser and his household used to entertain guests. A little of its grandeur remains – a vaulted ceiling, the curved wall of the tower – but the fireplace has been lost, the tools of the lightkeeper's trade on display instead of the trappings of the rich. (Apparently, the loft – known as the Fiddlers Galley by the keepers – was used mainly for the storing of ropes.) The Hall is these days dominated by a set of four large white 40-gallon tanks. At one time, there were twelve of them, all in place since 1874 and used to store the paraffin that fuelled the light for many decades. This was far cleaner than its predecessor colza oil, which had been in use since 1847. However, it still entailed a great deal of work for the lightkeepers. Every day they would trek up the stairs with cans in their hands in order to fill the reservoirs that supplied the tank. The stink of paraffin would accompany them every step of the way, permeating both their uniforms and the lighthouse walls. It was a task that only came to an end in 1975 when the paraffin lamp was replaced by a mercury vapour electric lamp. The smell of the light's former fuel, however, continued to hang around for quite some time after that, more constant even than the signal.

And still we climb, circling a heavy blue chain on our way, one that occupies the otherwise vacant centre of the staircase…

The next level is the Chamber, also known as the occasional keeper's quarters. There's a wooden dresser with a radio and clock, an old-fashioned red torch on its shelves. A leather armchair. A narrow, uncomfortable-looking bed with a striped blanket. A wardrobe and electric cooker. An old record player and television set. I reflect on these objects, revisiting the furnishing and decoration of my own teenage years as I did so.

Clutching handrails, I climb up the last twelve steel steps to where the lamp is situated. As I do so, it seems to me that time travel is precisely the effect

Kinnaird Head Lighthouse

Entering Kinnaird Head lighthouse is like going back in time. The steps are in place for the Fiddlers Galley (top left) and the foghorn air compressors (bottom left) are still polished and gleaming. The wireless and television would have dramatically added to the sounds the keepers would otherwise have heard – their own voices, the swish of sea or storm, and the cries of nearby birds.
HES Canmore SC2100722, SC2100735, SC2100721, SC2100731

that the engineer, Thomas Smith, who designed the original Kinnaird Head lighthouse, was seeking. The entire building is an attempt to straddle time, linking two distinct and separate eras in a structure that is unique, simultaneously a castle and lighthouse. The original impetus for its creation came from a whirl of storms that blew across Scotland in the early 1780s,[2] sinking many vessels and having a detrimental effect on the wealth of the Scottish merchant class. This may have inspired the suggestion made, in an account of Fraserburgh written in 1785, that a lighthouse built on the headland would prevent some of these shipwrecks taking place. Alexander Fraser, 15th Lord Saltoun, picked up on the idea, perceiving it as the means to preserve the castle's crumbling tower on his estate. He would also profit in other ways, collecting shipping dues from the vessels that sailed around this part of the coast.

It did not entirely work out for him. His plans were derailed by the actions of George Dempster, the MP for the Fife and Forfar Burghs, who in 1786 introduced a bill that initiated the Northern Lighthouse Board. The Act for Erecting Certain Lighthouses in the Northern Parts of Great Britain brought about the first organisation ever where the primary purpose was to manage and build lighthouses. The initial four lighthouses planned were Mull of Kintyre, Eilean Glas on Scalpay off the coast of Harris, North Ronaldsay in Orkney and Kinnaird Head. These were all built during the following few years, Lord Saltoun agreeing to the lighthouse being built on the headland he owned in exchange for an annual rent of £7 sterling with one and a half acres of land also being given to the trustees.

The building that came to stand on Kinnaird Head was largely the work of two men. Thomas Smith, a tinsmith and lamp-maker from Edinburgh, attended the very first meeting of the trustees for the Northern Lighthouse Board. He would have known some of them due to his work in the New Town of Edinburgh, where he was partly responsible not only for manufacturing iron railings and grilles but also for improving the quality of street lighting, finding

Kinnaird Head Lighthouse
Elevation drawing of the lantern at Kinnaird Head, complete with wind vane, c1901.
NLB Canmore DP352056

new ways of trapping beams and ensuring they were not sullied by the grime that was a feature of the oil lamps of the period. To this initial encounter, he brought something which would have been new to the merchants at the gathering for all that this was already used elsewhere in Europe – a model of a lighthouse parabolic reflector. In simple terms, this consisted of a whale oil lamp which was set in the middle of a reflector.[3] Once its wick was lit, the glow would be enhanced by being reflected in tiny squares of mirrored glass. On this occasion, Smith's suggestion was rejected. Largely because of Smith's lack of experience in the field, the trustees preferred to contact Ezekiel Walker, an English lighthouse builder and scientist, whose contribution to the Scottish lighthouse building tradition has been almost overlooked. Claiming he was only able to erect one of the four the Board had planned, Walker offered to 'give directions for the other three for fifty Guineas and instruct any person the trustees thought proper'. As a result of this, Thomas Smith was chosen for the role, becoming the first engineer of the Northern Lighthouse Board after an apprenticeship of around two months, working alongside Walker in Norfolk during that time. It was perhaps because of his lack of knowledge of the intricacies of stone construction that, while the lamp in Kinnaird Head designed by Smith was lauded by seamen as one of the most brilliant lights of all time, there were often problems with the masonry of the towers that were built. They crumbled; their wooden roofs decayed; dampness seeped within.

It was the next generation that began to deal with these concerns, more specifically Thomas Smith's stepson (and son-in-law) Robert Stevenson. He began his role in the company by assisting his stepfather in the building of the lighthouse at Pentland Skerries – together with the one on Pladda on the south coast of Arran – in the last decade of the eighteenth century. The founder of a family dynasty, he deputised for Thomas Smith from 1797, then became the sole engineer from 1808 till he retired in 1842. During

2 This includes the aftermath of the eruption of Laki in Iceland, which lasted for eight months from early June 1783. This caused hardship and extreme weather not only in that country but throughout much of the Northern Hemisphere. Among the phenomena reported were severe thunderstorms, fog and 'yellow snow'. This had its effect on shipping around the coast of Scotland and elsewhere.

3 As Thomas was said to be the owner of an Arctic whaling ship, this was an easy fuel to both obtain and promote.

KINNAIRD   HEAD

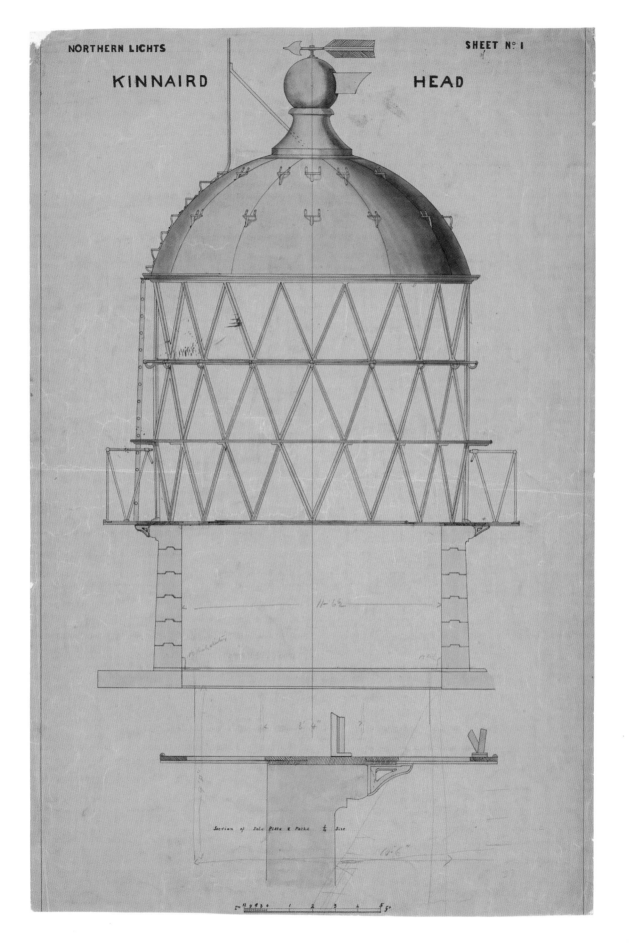

Section of Sole Plate & Path ½ Size

Kinnaird Head Lighthouse

Each morning the keeper would descend the long corkscrew of the stairs, seeing the chains and weight that had been the centre of his nightly cares …

Ian Cowe

that time, together with his foreman of works, Robert Selkirk, in 1824 he was responsible for redesigning the lighthouse at Kinnaird Head, which had become unsafe. It was this renovation that is responsible for the way the building looks today, with the lighthouse's winding staircase built through the interior of the former castle tower.

This was one reason why, after its light was doused for the last time in June 1991, Kinnaird Head lighthouse became a Property in Care looked after by Historic Scotland – now Historic Environment Scotland. Among the reasons for this were its direct connections with such significant historical figures as Thomas Smith and Robert Stevenson, and the importance of its geographical location at a strategic point near the entrance to the Moray Firth (the principal reason that the Commissioners chose to build their first lighthouse there). The lighthouse is managed as part of the Museum of Scottish Lighthouses, the reason why their employees are responsible for its upkeep and care.

Yet all this history is forgotten as I step into the force and flurry of the wind, Michael leading me out onto the gallery.[4] I circle it, looking out at the remaining parapet of the castle built by the Frasers many centuries earlier, the fishing boats and mix of vessels that cram Fraserburgh harbour, the red-roofed houses built nearby, the fish factories and other buildings that seem almost within reach, including one with its roof caved in. The strength of the wind

4 There was one occasion when I heard someone refer to this space as a 'pulpit'. This happened after the Northern Irish preacher and politician Rev Ian Paisley was seen stepping out there one day while paying a short visit to the Isle of Lewis during my teens. It is not known whether he was addressing anyone at the time. The seagulls were certainly not paying any attention.

is such that we only spend a few moments there before stepping back indoors again, Michael heaving the door behind him. It is at this point that his expertise is at its most valuable. He tells me how this light – created by the firm of Chance Brothers in Smethwick – was put in during the last days of 1902, becoming fully functional on 5 January 1903. It replaced the stationary one that had been there for the previous 50 years. David Alan Stevenson, grandson of Robert, was responsible for this change. As the new bi-order lens was over 10 feet (3m) tall and around 4 tons in weight, the entire light-room had to be enlarged and built around it. The walls were constructed in cast-iron with single holes to allow the space to be ventilated. At one point, Michael opened one or two of the decorative brass-stops by which these tiny hollows were hidden. The outside wind whistled on my fingertips as I pressed my hand against it. He explained why there were curtains draped around the inside of the lantern panes.

'If you didn't have them, there would be the danger of the lenses magnifying sunlight, causing fires. You lift them as the sun is about to go down, switching on the light at that time.'

He also spoke about how the keepers had to clean the lens every two days.

'That's because otherwise they'd have a coating of grease and oil. Especially in the days back when they used paraffin.'

I was invited to push the button to start the movement of the light, watching the twelve wheels revolve on a series of steel rollers, slowly and resolutely. 'They had to turn it by hand for sixteen nights one winter on the Monach Isles after the winding mechanism became jammed.'

There was also the paraffin vapour lamp fixed to the wall, its tip draped with an incandescent candle mantle.[5] The latter resembled a tiny piece of gossamer or lace, a wisp of bog-cotton one might find on the moor. When it was ignited, it was this delicate fragment that provided the lamp's glow, enlarged and magnified by the lenses and gleaming in the direction of the sea.

'I remember something like that,' I declared, telling Michael of the paraffin lamp that used to light up the bothan – the illegal drinking clubs in Ness I attended in my teenage years. There was a similar means of illumination in the building.

He pointed a finger, too, in the direction of the weathervane at the tower's crest, telling me it also served as a ventball, allowing the smoke and fumes to escape.

And then he solved the mystery of the chain hanging in the stairwell, the empty space that the steps to the light curled round.

'That's what keeps the reflectors moving. They're turned round and around by this red clockwork machine you see underneath. It's crammed with steel ball-bearings, each helping to carry the bulk of it. And that's driven by a dropping weight which pulls the gears of the mechanism. That's attached to the long chain you see in the middle of the stairs. It takes exactly 30 minutes to reach the bottom of the tower. That movement downwards keeping the reflectors moving.'

'And then?'

'You push this handle here to start the whole process going again.' He laughs. 'And if you fail to do that, if the weight touches the floor, an alarm and a light goes off, bringing your fellow-keepers up the stairs in minutes. It was one way you made sure you never nodded off. You'd lose your job if you did so. Go on.' He nods in my direction. 'Give it a try.'

It is at this point I fulfil one of my life's ambitions, one that might have been nurtured the day I went up the steps of the Butt of Lewis lighthouse with Bodach Dubh all those years before. I do as Michael said, gaining the satisfaction of listening to a ratcheting sound as the chain shifts and moves, heaving upwards, hearing, too, the loud clang of the weight echoing around me as it strikes, glad too that – if I fail to do this – there will not be the warning noise of a klaxon sounding to alert my imaginary colleagues of my failure to conduct the task …

5 Sometimes this was simply called the 'incandescent lamp'.

Chapter 3
Where Lies the Land?
The Revolutionary Eddystone Lighthouses

Where lies the land to which the ship would go?
Far, far ahead, is all her seamen know.

Arthur Hugh Clough, 'Where Lies the Land'

According to legend, the land beneath my neighbourhood lighthouse, the Butt of Lewis – or Rubha Robhanais – nearly vanished from its current location many centuries ago.

This occurred when the Vikings threaded rope through Sùil an Rubha, or the Eye of the Butt, a natural arch the seas have carved in the rock near the lighthouse's foundation. Their intention? To drag the entire Western Isles to the coastline of Norway, settling each rock and acre of land found at this western edge of their maps near their former homes. Their efforts were not entirely successful. Within a short time, the longships at the rear of this flotilla were making their way to the front to report the fracturing they had observed in the landscape of the Western Isles, which (allegedly) had been a single island until this moment in its history.

Eddystone Lighthouse, Plymouth, England

'The sea is so great, Lord, and my boat is so small,' was once uttered in the prayers of French sailors during a storm. The same is true of lighthouses – this nineteenth century engraving of the Eddystone lighthouse shows the tower under the weight and assault of waves.

© Liszt Collection/Bridgeman

'Barra's broken off at the end.'
'Uist – both North and South – have gone … '
'Even Harris is splitting off!'

It is a tale I sometimes thought of as a youngster, on days with the wind blowing round us shrieking and screaming. I would watch the lighthouse coming under the sway of a swathe of surf or foam, one that made the tower disappear for a moment or two, washed from sight. It reminded me of the magician's cloth – 'Abracadabra! Hocus pocus! Voila!'. There were moments when, under the full-blown fury of a storm, I expected the building to disappear forever, no longer remaining upright under the weight and impact of water. But then it emerged again from that onslaught of salt, still unchanged, still secure upon that promontory where it had stood for so many years. It looked as if Armageddon, the End of Days, the Apocalypse would have to come before the lighthouse would be rendered into powder and stone once again …[1]

Not so with the Eddystone lighthouse near Plymouth, where the first ever attempt to build a lighthouse on offshore rocks around these islands –

---

1 Actually, this was not as unlikely as it might have seemed. Former lightkeeper Archie MacEachern noted that often, when spring tides occurred, there was a distinct rumbling sound in Butt of Lewis lighthouse. After he left, they discovered that the sea cave below the lighthouse was beginning to collapse. Contractors filled in the cavity that had been created there with a special kind of cement in order to keep the structure upright.

The Eddystone Lighthouses

The phases of the Eddystone lighthouse as viewed by artist Andras Kaldor, culminating in the tower that stood upright to the challenge of these waters.

Bridgeman Images

or indeed anywhere else in the world – was made. Its originator was Henry Winstanley (1644–1703), an individual with some claim to be that age's 'David Copperfield' – the illusionist who once appeared to make the famous (failed) lighthouse the Statue of Liberty vanish from sight. Winstanley's home was a House of Fun to the paying public who entered its doors. Inside there were ghostly apparitions, distorting mirrors and a clockwork organ. He was also the owner of the Waterworks visitor attraction in London, where fireworks and spectacular water features were on display, including the 'Wonderful Barrel' which served different types of drinks – both hot and cold – from the same tap.

His ingenuity led to other achievements. He became the owner of five ships, two of them wrecked on the Eddystone Rocks. It was this that led him to undertake the singular task for which his name is known today – erecting a lighthouse on one of the most dangerous reefs in the British Isles.

It was an ambitious and strenuous plan, beset by many difficulties and problems. One was the very substance and form of the rock itself, gneiss. There was only a small sloping surface on which a lighthouse could be built. The nature of the gneiss was such that during the first year they only succeeded in hacking 12 holes into its surface for the iron stanchions used to embed the building into the stone. During the second year of construction, 1697, Winstanley was caught up in the last few months of the Nine Years War. He was kidnapped by a French privateer and brought to the court of the Sun King, Louis XIV, who – after

seeking to persuade him to work for the French crown – allowed Winstanley the freedom to return to his labours. The third year was more successful. With workmen now living on site, Winstanley was set to create a building that he claimed would 'stand forever as one of the world's most artistic pieces of work'.

It did not tame the reef for long. First lit on 14 November 1698, this ornate and elaborate building met its end on 26 November 1703 during what was described by Daniel Defoe as, 'The Greatest, the Longest in Duration, the widest in Extent, of all the Tempests and Storms that History gives any Account of since the Beginning of Time.' This was a weather event known to us as 'The Great Storm', which had a cataclysmic effect on the south of England. It left thousands dead, one-fifth of the English fleet underwater, and many acres of land flooded under a tidal surge.

It also did what I sometimes imagined waves doing to the Butt of Lewis lighthouse in my childhood. It washed the Eddystone lighthouse away, together with Winstanley, who was ensconced inside that night, both his life and his creation coming to a sudden and crashing end …

It was fire that performed a similar task next time – a whirl of sparks and flame, a billowing of smoke.

The substitute for Winstanley's elaborate structure came about for good reason. Whereas no ships had been sunk in the vicinity of the reef during the five years his tower had stood beaming light from the rock, within two days of its destruction, a merchant ship sank, with 60 lives being lost. This tragedy alone demonstrated the need for a replacement, and work began on it immediately.

However, it was a very different construction from the previous model. John Rudyard (or Rudyerd), hitherto a London dealer in silks and other textiles, had discerned one particular truth from past experience. He understood that one reason Winstanley's tower had tumbled below the waves was because of its sheer artistry. Instead of a glass-walled lantern, wrought-iron and wooden vane and the other intricacies that had marked Winstanley's creation, Rudyard devised a smooth tapering tower with as few

Stone-Cutting, Oreston

Famous for its limestone quarries, Oreston on the shoreline of the Cattewater is now a suburb of Plymouth. The masons who were employed here were responsible for cutting the stone that later formed the Eddystone lighthouse.

From *The Illustrated London News*, 30 August 1879 – Look and Learn / Illustrated Papers Collection / Bridgeman Images

projections, bulges and bumps as possible, one that would ascend to a height of 28 metres. He was assisted in all of this by shipwrights from a naval dockyard. They helped to line Rudyard's lighthouse with pitch-caulked oak planks, normally used in sailing ships for waterproofing. He even raised a kind of wooden mast in the centre of the tower, attempting to strengthen its structure and ensure it was wind, weather and wave-tight, unlike its predecessor. While there were early difficulties, especially in the manner in which the oak planks became worm-eaten, it stood for nearly half a century, shining its beam for the first time in 1709.

And then the night of the towering inferno …

In the early hours of 2 December 1755, fire broke out in the lantern room. It did not take long to spread through the remainder of the building – the disadvantages of using wood in such a construction all too plain to be seen (although fire remained a constant hazard even in later stone lighthouses, badly damaging, for instance, Skerryvore, Chicken Rock and Bell Rock at various points in the twentieth century).

The person selected to build the next replacement was a Yorkshireman called John Smeaton (1724–92). It was a task the authorities were keen to undertake immediately. The British were about to embark on yet another conflict with France, the Seven Years War beginning in 1756, a year after Rudyard's lighthouse had burnt down. The Royal Navy wanted to avoid the possibility of any of its fleet colliding into the underwater reef. John Smeaton, who had been elected a fellow of the Royal Society in 1753, proved to be the best person for the project.

Right from the beginning, this was a different approach. It was not the work of a magician like Winstanley. Neither did it employ timber as in Rudyard's design. The only similarity Smeaton's structure shared with wood was that it adopted the shape of an oak tree, one that was 'broad at the base, curves inward at the waist, becomes narrower towards the top'. This was, however, to be fashioned from stone, which he believed would possess the resilience to stand up against the continual force and hammering of the sea. Bringing together a team of 24 workers, half of whom were stonemasons, the other 12 labourers from the Cornish mines, Smeaton began to put together a tower that would prove to be more durable than anything that had been created before this – the stone blocks dovetailing together in horizontal layers in a fashion only previously found

Eddystone Lighthouse 1887

The final tower – which, to use the words of William Wordsworth in his poetic tribute to Grace Darling, the lightkeeper's daughter who rescued survivors off the Northumberland coast in 1838, brought 'Hope to the hopeless, to the dying life'. The stump of Smeaton's tower is in the background.

in the trade of carpentry. He also employed marble 'joggles', a notch or projection in one piece of material which is fitted to another in a second piece to prevent one from slipping on the other. There were also wooden pins known as 'trenails' employed to connect the layers vertically. All of this was shaped and fashioned on land before being shipped to the rock, where each separate block was lifted onto the building site. During the course of three years, in the region of 1,500 separate stones were brought to the Eddystone reef, a collective weight of nearly 1,000 tons – an achievement all the more remarkable because Smeaton sometimes had to compete with the attentions of the press-gang for his workforce. At one time, they were all taken en masse to fight in the conflict and only claimed back from the navy with great difficulty.

Despite such obstacles, the building of the lighthouse was successful, lit for the first time on 16 October 1759. In use for over a century, perched upon a rock, the tower was only abandoned in the 1870s when it was discovered that waves were eroding its base and a cave opening up below its foundations. It was as a result of this that a fourth Eddystone lighthouse had to be constructed by James Douglas (1826–1898). Completed in 1882, it still stands today, occupying a neighbouring rock to the one occupied by a stub of Smeaton's tower. The upper part of the latter is still erect as a memorial on Plymouth Hoe. It is right that it is. Despite having been tall and imposing upon that rock only temporarily, its role in history has been permanent and long-lasting.

For there were others who watched the agonies and ecstasies involved in the construction of the Eddystone lighthouses, seeking some awareness of the lessons learned. Among them were those who wished to build a lighthouse on the Inchcape Rock, some 12 miles off the coast of Arbroath…

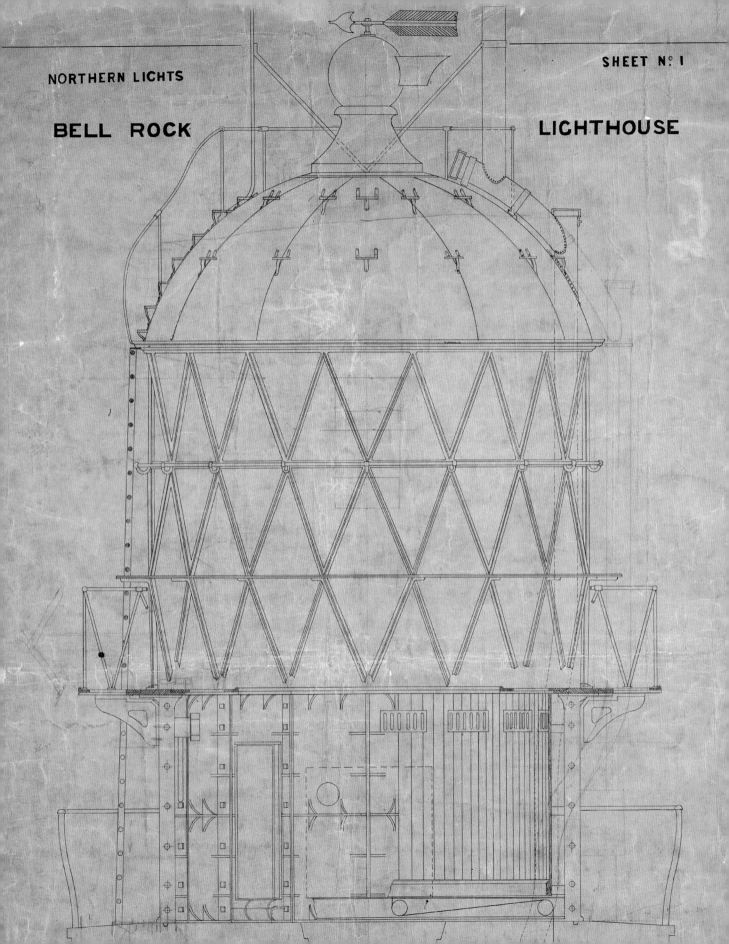

NORTHERN LICHTS

BELL ROCK

LICHTHOUSE

Chapter 4
A Light Dawned
The Story of Bell Rock

The local situation and circumstances of Scotland necessarily directed the genius of its people to the pursuit of nautical affairs.

Robert Stevenson, *An Account of the Bell Rock Light-house*

Many winter days are gloomy but, even within them, there are sometimes moments when the sky is cloudless, and light can be sharp and clean. The day in early December when I arrived in Arbroath wasn't one of them. There was no hint of glint or beam dancing on the grey waters of the North Sea; no shimmer or sparkle on shop windows; no relief from the shadows that fell on Dishlandtown Street and Keptie Street that afternoon as I walked through the town, losing my way as this son of the Hebrides all too frequently does, never having had to acquire much of a sense of direction in either my childhood or youth. Back then there were only around two routes to select from. It didn't give me much opportunity to lose myself – or find myself again.

Bell Rock Lighthouse, Angus A Listed

From a sheet of paper to reality – an elevation drawing of the proposed upgrade to the lantern at Bell Rock dated 1 March 1900 and signed by David Alan Stevenson before it was transformed into a beam that can be seen some 18 miles away.

NLB Canmore DP352565

That morning I was en route to one of the buildings that, together with its famous abbey, gave this community much of its standing in the world – the white and pristine Signal Tower only a short distance away from the train station. For all the cloud-ridden nature of the day, as I strolled towards it, I could see the Bell Rock lighthouse itself, tall and spectral at the far edge of the horizon, its pale shade contrasting with the dark forms of the seven shags standing like attendees at a funeral on a nearby sea-wall. They stretched wings to shake and dry their feathers, appearing to discuss the bitterness of the day or the possibility of catching fish, ignoring the presence of the tower behind them. Built in 1811 on Inchcape Rock, three years earlier than its shoreline companion, the lighthouse seemed to me a distant miracle, its existence challenging the outrage and fury of both wind and wave that must have attempted a thousand times to blow the structure down, grinding and smashing the courses of stone out of which it was constructed.

The two towers are very much the bedrock of the Northern Lighthouse Board. They even feature on that organisation's own distinctive tartan on display in its offices on George Street in Edinburgh. Symbols and allusions are stitched into this square of cloth. Much of it is the blue-grey colour of the North Sea. The sett or thread count of 290 threads represents the 290 feet of railway coming to an end towards the west of Inchcape Rock, at a location called Hope's Wharf, where material was taken for the construction of the lighthouse.[1] Two of the diagonal lines on this tartan are said to represent horizons. There is 'Horizon 2' stitched in a darker thread where the Signal Tower stands, its lantern the criss-cross of a red beam. On the other side of the segment is 'Horizon 1', which is the line dominated by the Bell Rock lighthouse itself. The 90 courses of stone of which the tower was constructed are signified by 90 stitches, erect and upright too, on the dark strands that suggest the Inchcape Rock. With its mix of shades and colours, the tartan acts as a memorial that commemorates the thousands of lives that have been lost over the centuries on this area of coastline, especially on the Inchcape Rock. It also acts as a reminder of the two men who, according to Robert Stevenson's own account, died during the construction of the Bell Rock lighthouse over two hundred years ago.

And so, I step into the courtyard that leads to the Signal Tower. It incorporates a number of other buildings that until 1973 served as houses for the fishermen of the area. Nowadays, the cottages act as two exhibition centres – one defined as the Maritime Trade Cottage; the other the Fishing Industry Cottage. I nosed my way into the two of them, taking a quick note of the displays before I scurried out again. Neither was the focus of my interest. Instead, it was the immaculate structure that dominated the square. I pushed the button and the door opened, ushering me into the mysteries of the building. Entering, I was all too glad to escape the storm that was beginning to puff and blow. I was aware that, even if it were possible, this was not a day when voyages to the Bell Rock were going to be on offer. Any vessel making its way through these waters would have to crash through troughs, surge over crests and peaks, with spindrift and spray drenching those on board as it crossed over the force and fathoms of the North Sea. I would have to be content with this onshore, domesticated version of the Bell Rock tower.

The welcome I received from Museum Officer Karen Clarke as she introduced the exhibits in the Signal Tower Museum made it easy to feel this way. The first exhibit we encountered portrayed in both words and pictures the story of the Inchcape Rock, a sharp reef of red sandstone, roughly 425m in length, that imperilled the ships that sailed in this part of the ocean. Its existence bedevilled the lives of mariners. Sail east of it and your vessel was open to the fierce storms of the North Sea. Sail closer to land and there was the danger you might end up on shoreline rocks. Over its surface, the seas roared and surged like a series of question marks, testing the solidity and safety of your vessel, making every voyage in these waters a dangerous dilemma for both sailors and fishermen. It was because of this – legend says – that in the fourteenth century the Bishop of Arbroath decided to fix a bell to the reef's surface, providing it with the alternative name by which the rock is known today. In 1815, the Poet Laureate Robert Southey wrote a ballad, *The Inchcape Rock*, about this tale:

> The holy Abbot of Aberbrothok
> Had placed that bell on the Inchcape Rock;
> On a buoy in the storm it floated and swung,
> And over the waves its warning rung.
> When the Rock was hid by the surge's swell.

He tells the story of how a pirate – Ralph the Rover – removed this bell from its perch, only to suffer some dramatic poetic justice in return for his actions. As he perishes below the heft of water:

> One dreadful sound could the Rover hear;
> A sound as if with the Inchcape Bell,
> The Devil below was ringing his knell.

It was the sheer volume of the rock's toll on both ships and human life that first prompted thoughts about the possibility of placing a warning light there. For all that his efforts were not supported by the Northern Lighthouse Board, Royal Navy Captain Joseph Brodie pursued this goal on a few occasions in the last years of the eighteenth century, only to be doomed to disappointment with the lamp being either doused by waves or swept away by storms. In December 1799, the attitudes of the Commissioners were forced to alter, as both they and the public observed that over 70 vessels had been lost after a storm from the north-east. Their concerns hardened in 1803, when the HMS *York* also went missing with all its men drowned. This, too, was believed to have been the result of a direct collision with the rock.

1 Rt Hon Charles Hope, Lord President of the Court of Session, was the individual responsible for initiating the building of the lighthouse in 1803, when the first bill to Parliament was presented.

The Inchcape Rock by Peter Graham

Peter Graham's painting of 1908 illustrates the moment when in the savagery and centre of a storm, the devil rang his knell.

Leicester Museum & Art Gallery

These events caused them to ponder the possibility of creating their own version of the Eddystone lighthouse, even though Bell Rock had certain disadvantages over that edifice. It was noted that the base of the tower near Plymouth 'was barely covered by the tide at high water while Bell Rock was barely uncovered at low water' – the latter a fact that still astonishes those who come to visit it even today. Nevertheless, two men – Robert Stevenson (1772–1850) and John Rennie (1761–1821) – came up with a similar solution to this dilemma, a round stone tower which was not unlike Smeaton's sturdy construction down south. John Rennie was appointed chief engineer and Robert Stevenson his deputy – a fact that Karen reminded me of as we walked around the Signal Tower.

'Don't forget Rennie. He's always missed out in accounts of Bell Rock.'

Conscious that a great rivalry existed between the two men and their descendants, I jotted this down in my notebook, moving to the next room as I did so. It was Stevenson's account that prevailed here – as it does in most writings about Bell Rock. There are reasons for this. It is his bookplates that largely illustrate the process by which the tower was built. John Rennie only visited the rock on two occasions while the work was going on, while, in contrast, Stevenson was a consistent presence. It is also true that Stevenson earned the respect of many by not making the building of the lighthouse his first priority. Instead, his emphasis was on constructing a barracks beside where the tower would stand, increasing the safety of the men who were employed on it as well as reducing their travel time to and from their work. It was a structure on which much of the progress of the Bell Rock lighthouse was based. Eventually, it was 45-foot-tall (almost 14m), housing not only the artificers – those who were responsible for boring holes into the rock – but also providing space for a smithy, a kitchen and a room for Stevenson himself.

It was after this that the cut stone began to arrive, the pieces designed for a giant mosaic of sandstone for the tower's interior and a jigsaw of harder stone for its exterior, each hewn and dovetailed to a perfect fit by a team of 60 stonecutters in Arbroath. For this work, John Rennie deserves most credit. He took Smeaton's design for the Eddystone lighthouse and improved on it, securing these pieces to the centre of the tower, ensuring that if it was struck by the weight of powerful waves, the force would make the stones cleave together instead of tugging them apart. He also added small holes into which 16–26 inch (40–65cm) trenails were placed, each one of these pegs designed to continue 4 inches into the level below, each course in these lower levels consisting of 123 stones. The stones were shipped to the rock in small sailing boats, lifted upwards by the cranes they had on site. By the end of 1808, after two years' work, the tower was a little over 5 feet tall (1.5m). The work was slow and patient, the fragmentary pieces of the Bell Rock lighthouse taking time, perseverance and effort to fit into place.

This was less true of the following two years. With each layer, they were moving slowly away from the reach of tide and wave. They also required fewer and fewer stones as the tower both narrowed and was hollowed out to allow space for the rooms within. In addition, in an attempt to speed construction, the stones in the upper part no longer required to be bored for trenails as they had been in the lower levels. The jigsaw could be completed without this. The floors – or ceilings – all conformed to the basic pattern of 123 stones. Set into the exterior walls, they, too, were courses in their own right.[2]

This is not to claim that the construction was without problems. After the winter of 1808–9, parts of the railway tracks that were such a vital component of the lighthouse's creation had been dislodged or damaged, sometimes by the sea itself but just as often by boulders flung upwards by the waves. These had to be both replaced and improved in the early days of spring. Despite this, progress was being made. One of the diagrams illustrating the building of Bell Rock displays a rope bridge hanging between the barracks and the tower. This was put into position when the latter structure had reached the dizzy heights of 10 feet (3m). With time, this was replaced by a timber

bridge which was itself able to support a crab-winch capable of raising stones. It was one of a variety of cranes, winches and other lifting equipment the tower began to sprout over the next couple of years. On land, they were also aided by an animal which possessed legendary power and strength. 'That's Bassey,' Karen said, indicating the picture of the skeleton of a horse displayed on a wall. 'Over three years, she brought nearly three thousand cut blocks of stone from her work-place to the harbour. Over 2,083 tons.'

Karen pointed out something else to me as we walked round the Signal Tower Museum – evidence again and again of the humanity of Robert Stevenson. As the tower grew in height, so did the man's moral stature. He showed, for instance, great interest in the safety and welfare of the workforce. One of the unfortunate by-products of the increase in the scale and stature of the tower is that, as it grew, so did the number of accidents. In August 1808, 18-year-old James Scott drowned. On 30 June 1809, Michael Wishart's legs were broken when a crane toppled over. On 17 July 1809, William Walker was killed when a large rock toppled on him. During each of these occasions, Robert Stevenson displayed a sensitivity quite exceptional for an employer during this period. He not only visited injured workers in hospital but also ensured both they and the grieving relatives of those who had died were cared for. Discovering, for example, that, with his father a prisoner-of-war, young James Scott was the one who provided financially for his family, Robert Stevenson offered Jame's 14-year-old brother the dead man's place in the workforce. It was a practical measure that meant a great deal to those who had lost a loved one, a mixture of the industry and human care that went into the creation of the 90 courses of stone, amounting to 36m in height. On 30 July 1810, the last layer was set in place, the final stone accompanied by the words of Robert Stevenson's benediction when he declared: 'May the Great Architect of the Universe, under whose blessing this perilous work has prospered, preserve it as a guide to the mariner.'

In February 1811, the lamp was lit and the tower habitable, allowing three keepers to reside there for six

2 For practical reasons, Stevenson abandoned the domed ceilings used in Smeaton's tower.

Bell Rock Lighthouse
The construction of Bell Rock, from Robert Stevenson's *An Account of the Bell Rock Light-house*, engraved by William Miller.
HES Canmore DP089757, DP089759

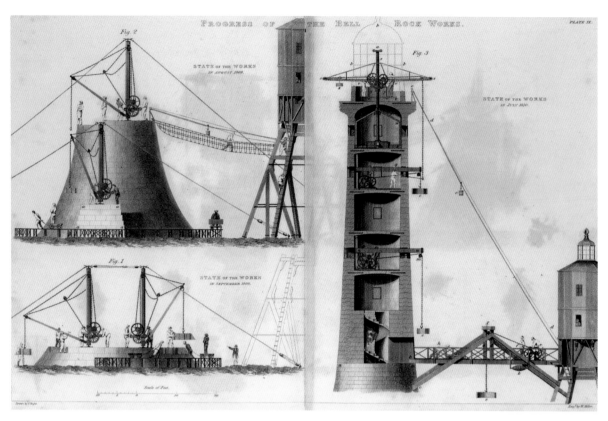

PROGRESS OF THE BELL ROCK WORKS.

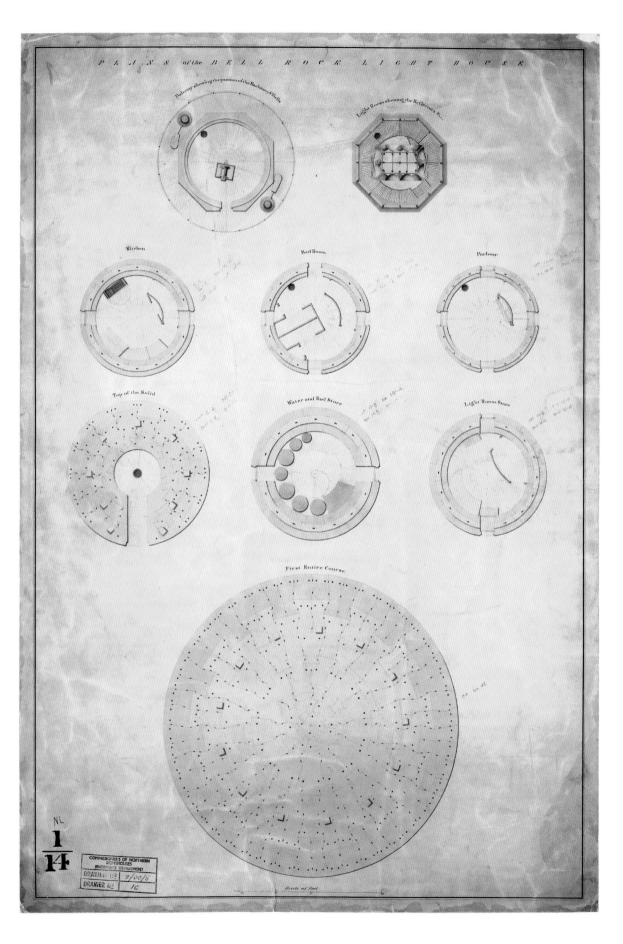

Balcony shewing the position of the Machinery & Bells

Light Room shewing the Reflectors &c.

Kitchen

Bed Room

Parlour

Top of the Solid

Water and Fuel Store

Light Room Store

First Entire Course

Scale of Feet

weeks at a time followed by two weeks ashore. Over time this changed to two months on then one month off, and by the 1970s the standard pattern operated by the Northern Lighthouse Board for remote or rock stations was one month at the light followed by one month off. This continued until the last manned light, Fair Isle South, was automated at the end of March 1998.[3] With the keepers identified as A, B or C, their daily periods of work could be outlined as follows:

Time	Day 1	Day 2	Day 3
00.00–04.00	A	C	B
04.00–12.00	B	A	C
12.00–16.00	C	B	A
16.00–20.00	A	C	B
20.00–24.00	B	A	C

As a result of this, each man had to do 24 hours of work over three days.[4]

Occasionally, too, if someone were ill or experiencing family difficulties, a supernumerary had to be called in to replace the individual concerned. It was one of the areas where the Signal Tower – completed in 1813 – had its own role. Above its lantern, a copper signal ball would be raised each day between 9 and 10am – or 1 and 2pm in foggy weather. This action was imitated by those on Bell Rock, a sign that their signal had been seen. There was one occasion in 1868 when the lightkeepers failed to complete their signal through a lapse in memory. It resulted in a heavy fine of £2 to cover the expense of sending out a boat. For all that they must have grudged this, the lightkeepers may have been – on balance – glad to pay this sum. The dwellings around the Signal Tower provided homes for both themselves and their families. They also functioned as stores and sources of information.[5] Alarm, too, could be signalled by those in the lighthouse to those on land.

Clearly, in the early years, this system for summoning help could be problematic. On days and

---

3 The Northern Lighthouse Board is now responsible for 206 automated lights. Prior to automation there were 91 manned lighthouses in the hands of NLB, in addition to many more which were unmanned.
4 According to Calum Macaulay, at one time lightkeepers did three hours' duty at a time with an additional three hours looking after the foghorn if this was required. In later years, the Northern Lighthouse Board adopted the four hour model noted above.
5 See Chapter 7 for other ways in which the pole for the copper signal ball might be used.

Bell Rock Lighthouse previous pages
Robert Stevenson and John Rennie's Bell Rock lighthouse plan and elevation engineering drawings c1800.
NLB Canmore DP039993, DP077864

Bell Rock Lighthouse Signal Tower, Angus **A Listed**
Used at one time for – what must have been – the most outlandish council housing in the country, the buildings were finally transformed into a museum in 1974, one of the highlights of a visit to Arbroath.
HES Canmore SC358171

nights when storms thundered and raged, it was not always possible to retrieve a man from a rock or island when a signal wasn't returned. These circumstances only altered with the use of helicopters, a development which according to keeper Calum Macaulay was the greatest and most welcome change that took place throughout his working years. 'It meant there was an immediate response to the issue. You didn't have to wait till the weather changed and you could send out a boat.'

The demands of the watch-keeping schedule meant that three lightkeepers had to be employed at one time at a remote lighthouse – a principal, principal assistant and assistant – though many shore-based lights might have only two. As well as the mundane requirements of work shifts, a more dramatic story was sometimes given as a reason for this. In Trinity House's[6] Smalls lighthouse near Pembrokeshire in 1801, there were only two lightkeepers. The relationship between them was – allegedly – difficult and tense. During their spell on duty, one died. Rather than run the risk of being charged with his murder by depositing his associate deep within the waves, the other decided to preserve the corpse. (In some accounts, he did this by fastening the dead man's body in a chest which he fashioned from the wooden framework of the lighthouse dwellings and hanging this outside the tower's walls.) He was then forced to carry on his duties alone until others arrived to relieve him, their examination on arrival clearing him of any suspicion of killing his companion. This story was apparently one of the sources for the recent film *The Lighthouse*, directed by Robert Eggers and featuring Willem Dafoe and Robert Pattinson as

---

6 Trinity House has a number of different functions, but in this context, it is principally the General Lighthouse Authority responsible for those structures standing in England, Wales, the Channel Islands and Gibraltar.

two lightkeepers on a remote island going slowly and irrecoverably mad.

Even with three people, there were moments when there could be tension. One man, whom I knew and often met in Shetland, the late Lawrence Tulloch, wrote about this in his account of his eight years working in Scotland's lighthouses. In *On the Rocks: A Lightkeeper's Tale*, he mentions the experience of being awakened by the screams of one of his fellow-keepers who was suffering from nightmares after his involvement in action during the Second World War.[7] The roaring and punching was so intense that, occupying the top bunk, Lawrence 'literally hit the ceiling with his head' in alarm and fear each time the man cried out in his sleep.

According to Lawrence, there is also no doubt that places as isolated and confined as Bell Rock intensified petty enmities and annoyances. He describes one individual whom he met within the six principal

rooms where they were confined with the following warm and glowing words: 'At first glance he radiated neither charisma nor charm. As it turned out, my first impressions were accurate if a little generous to the man.'

He goes on to note how the other man never left him alone, even remaining alongside him when he tried to bathe – an act that, for various reasons, outlined below, had to be performed inside their shared kitchen.

It is clear from both this and other writings that Bell Rock's structure was not foolproof. There were dangers embedded in its design. Lawrence states that the Northern Lighthouse Board became acutely aware of one issue after two incidents took place involving similar rock lighthouses. The first of these occurred on 16 March 1954 when Skerryvore was almost destroyed

---

7 There appears to have been a relatively high proportion of the men stationed on lighthouses who suffered from the effects of their wartime experiences. Whether this was by accident, design, or indeed individual choice on their part is unclear.

Bell Rock Lighthouse
The nineteenth century interior was modernised in 1964 to meet the changing demands of lighthouse life.
Ian Cowe

by fire, which probably started in the kitchen. After a rather providential escape, the keepers spent the remainder of that evening perched on the rock until they were rescued by chance the following morning. The second occurred on the night of 23 December 1960, when a similar rock lighthouse at Chicken Rock on the Isle of Man was seriously damaged by flames, its hollow tower acting like a chimney, creating an enormous updraft. Fortunately all its keepers survived. There was another problem with Bell Rock that was obvious from the moment it was first occupied. Its structure shook and trembled under the impact of waves: an unfortunate by-product of the rigidity built into the structure by Stevenson and Rennie. There would have been times when, drenched by spray, it must have resembled the lighthouse mentioned in *Little Dorrit* by Charles Dickens, 'white, haunting the seaboard, as if it were the ghost of an edifice that once had colour and rotundity', dripping 'melancholy tears after its late buffeting by waves'.

There were additional difficulties. For all that the building had been praised for its luxury in the early and mid-nineteenth century by the likes of

Sir Walter Scott and the author of *The Coral Island*, R M Ballantyne,[8] the tower was increasingly becoming outdated and uncomfortable. Some improvements were made to the lighthouse in 1963, and it was electrified the following year. After the incidents that occurred in Chicken Rock and Skerryvore, all that was combustible was removed. The tower became no longer dependent on coal, and a gas stove was installed instead. The oil and coal stores in the bottom two floors were removed. The old fog-signal, internal to these towers and regarded as both explosive and dangerous, was removed. The mahogany in the bedroom was stripped down and adjustable bunks put in place instead. The library was removed.

8 Ballantyne wrote a book entitled *The Lighthouse: The Story of a Great Fight Between Man and Sea* based largely on the fortnight in the mid-1860s he spent on Bell Rock.

The Lighthouse Tender SS Pharos by D M D McQuade

One of the many incarnations of the Northern Lighthouse Board ship the *Pharos* that have visited Bell Rock over the years – this fourth incarnation was a paddle steamer built by William Fairbairn & Son in 1846.

HES TRH021

All the wooden hatches and ladders were also taken from the tower and replaced with non-combustible materials. Despite these precautions the Bell was severely damaged by fire in September 1987, during automation. All three keepers, who had stayed on while changes were being made to automate the light, were rescued.

There were other changes. A new lens – much smaller than Stevenson's hyper-radial lens that had been the basis of its lantern since 1902 – was installed, powered now by electricity. This created space to install new water tanks, increasing the storage from 260 to 690 gallons (1,180 to 3,135 litres). It also allowed space

for a back-up lantern if the other failed. While most of these alterations were welcome, there were some new difficulties introduced with the improvements. The library may have been an outmoded luxury, but it also offered some space and privacy for the men. Now the kitchen and sitting room occupied the same limited space.

In his book, my friend Lawrence Tulloch goes into detail about the problems of being employed at Bell Rock, even during the 1970s. He is fulsome about the toilet facilities there, especially as there were still tight limits on the amount of fresh water available to the men. Going to the toilet involved a great deal of energy and forward planning on the keepers' part. If they needed to urinate, the keepers generally went out onto the gallery. This was relatively simple and straightforward on a dry, calm night. However, the task was rendered much more complex when a wet and showery wind gusted round the tower. Otherwise, it necessitated hitching your trousers down and reversing through the toilet door. Tensions between the men were sometimes heightened by other issues. Many of these involved the confinement of the kitchen-cum-sitting room-cum-bathroom – the fact that there was only one area in which they could relax, one TV (and one station) that could be watched. This space was only 11 feet (3.4m) in diameter, an area where men could go up and down but any lateral movement was limited. 'On every floor,' Lawrence notes, 'the walls were covered in a bewildering mass of wiring and plumbing. Pipes were colour coded. Pipes carrying diesel oil were painted brown, fresh water was white, saltwater blue,[9] paraffin red and waste pipes black.'

It could all hardly be described as homely.

Instead, life there involved great complexities and complications. Clearly, it is difficult to adjust and transform a building constructed in the early years of the nineteenth century to the realities of twentieth – and indeed twenty-first – century life and all its requirements. The fact that the Northern Lighthouse Board and Bell Rock succeeded – to any degree – in adapting to these changes shows what a remarkable

building Robert Stevenson and John Rennie created. It reveals, too, why Bell Rock has been imitated in the structure of most rock lighthouses, such as Skerryvore and Dubh Artach, not only in this country but throughout the world.

It also underlines why it is the tower most celebrated in the offices of the Northern Lighthouse Board in Edinburgh. It is, for instance, the bust of its principal creator, Robert Stevenson, taken from the Bell Rock library, that can be seen in the entrance hall. It is a picture of Bell Rock, shrouded by spindrift and saltwater, that greets you at the door. It is the furniture that was once found within the tower that can now be discovered in its boardroom. And, of course, the miniature lighthouse which flashes over George Street from above the doorway is a model of the Bell Rock lighthouse.

It is the legacy of that building, even in terms of the human decency with which Robert Stevenson attempted to deal with those who were employed in its creation, that those involved in the Northern Lighthouse Board hope to enshrine and pass on to their employees today.

9 This was in place because of the existence of something that Lawrence describes as a 'strange-looking contraption in the tower'. This involved a process which was designed to turn sea water into fresh water. 'Apparently', Lawrence pointed out, 'it worked well but a serious snag became evident when it was discovered it took more than a gallon of diesel to produce one gallon of fresh water'.

Chapter 5
On Stormy Nights
Life and Death in Scotland's Lighthouses

How can you tell a lightkeeper has just entered the room? He always walks round it in a curve.

Lawrence Tulloch, author of *On the Rocks: A Lightkeeper's Tale* (private conversation)

There were a few nail-biting moments during Ian Duff's 17 years of life as a lightkeeper.

But first he had to be accepted for a post with the Northern Lighthouse Board. For all that he had always dreamed of being a lightkeeper, there were years when there seemed no possibility of ever becoming a member among its ranks. A pupil of Elgin Academy in Morayshire, he was the eldest of five children. His family circumstances left him little opportunity of fulfilling his ambition, he simply had to work from an early age. As a result, he obtained a job in a whisky distillery near his home, employed by both Glen Grant and Macallan. It was only when the last of these two made him and others redundant that the possibility of becoming a lightkeeper arose. In 1976, at the age of 28, he applied and was accepted, becoming a member of a service where, looking back, he 'loved every moment' of his experience.

Fair Isle (South) Lighthouse, Shetland B Listed
The tallest lighthouse in the Shetland Isles, storm and sea provide more than a little drama to both the building and its immediate location, its gleam often turning southward to North Ronaldsay and Orkney.

David Chapman / Alamy Stock Photo

This is not to say that there were not a few nervous instances during his years of employment, working at lighthouses as varied and far apart as Skerryvore, Duncansby Head, Pladda and Fair Isle. Sometimes these came from grappling with the natural world. On Christmas Eve in 1983 during his time on Duncansby Head, its cliffs a giddy 200 feet over the sea, he recalled wrestling with the garage doors outside the tower, all too aware that the power of the wind was likely to lift the roofs of these precast buildings and whirl them away. 'It shook my wife and I, taking us off our feet and dumped us down later, as if it was playing with us.'

And then there were incidents at sea, such as the time he journeyed – more than a shade anxiously – on the *Grace Darling*, the lighthouse boat to Muckle Flugga at the top of Unst in Shetland. It is a place that I have stepped towards on a few occasions, dodging the swirling wings of great and arctic skuas that swoop down to graze the tops of human heads if they dare to venture near nests occupied by their chicks. The sea-voyage to Muckle Flugga, as the former skipper of the *Grace Darling*, Jonathan Wills,[1] informed his readers in

---

1 Jonathan also tells a few stories about Sandy Wylie, an energetic ALK (or Assistant Light Keeper) who swam around the nearby stacks and skerries. Jonathan believes he landed on them all: Peerie Flugga, Cliff Skerry, Tipta Skerry, Pulsa Stack, Rumblings and Vesta Skerry, noting he 'didn't do it in a wanny, wisely picking his weather and his tides, but he did do it and he did it, I am reliably informed, wrapped in a Union Jack which he intended to unfurl on the peak of Vesta Skerry. He was foiled by the sharp beaks of the gannets – being in his bare feet he was unable to get past them.'

an article, could be a gut-churning experience. He notes that while he was 'cautious about tides':

> Flugga Sound was still an unpleasant surprise. It had a violent race that I found extremely alarming until Lowrie [Edwardson, a veteran who had experienced 36 years in the role] explained you could almost always avoid the worst of it by making a detour. This commotion in the ocean was caused by the action of tide against swell and sea, producing those short, steep waves that sank so many homeward-bound sixareens[2] in centuries gone by. If you studied your tides you could usually get to Da Rock, even in a southerly gale. Surprisingly, a gale from the right direction could flatten the sea enough to allow you to attempt a landing.

Yet, for all his travails on the *Grace Darling*, sailing out from Burrafirth to Muckle Flugga, there is no doubt about the moment that made Ian Duff most edgy and anxious. This involved the lighthouse that both he and others, including Brian Johnson, a lighthouse engineer from Shetland, consider the most impressive in the waters around Scotland: Skerryvore. The tallest of our towers, it is – like its nearby counterpart, Dubh Artach – pounded by 60 foot waves that often surge upwards around Tiree from the depths in the southern end of the Minch.

It was one of these waves that did the damage, the might of spume and spindrift breaking off the rotor blade on a small helicopter which landed on the Skerryvore helipad in 1978 to take an injured lightkeeper off the rock. Both Ian and his friend and fellow lightkeeper the late Gordon MacDonald from Coll looked at the scene with horror before they rushed to the wrecked aircraft. First they made sure the pilot and the injured man were all right. As they were whipped by one wave after another, the next thought came to mind. They knew they had to lash the damaged helicopter down to the surface of the pad, mooring it to the rock in case a flurry of wind or sea-water might do more damage, sweeping it away from the narrow space in which it stood. They spooled out rope, looped it round the cockpit, tail and rotor-blades, ensuring that it could not be shifted

2 The traditional six-handed Shetland fishing boat.

whatever force and fury that day's storm might bring. As soon as this task was completed, they contacted the coastguard service, letting them know what had occurred. A moment later that team were back in touch, telling them they would be sending out another helicopter, both to rescue the other two men and to lift the broken, wounded aircraft from the rock before any further harm was done.

Ian recalled the next stage of the operation with wonder, his voice softening as he recalled what his friend Gordon did next.

'He went to get a few more long pieces of rope, splicing them to ensure they were all exactly the same length. Few men could have done the likes of that, worked with that kind of precision. He was an amazing man. Very, very skilled.'

With this work he spun a makeshift cradle, fastened and tied to the broken helicopter's length and breadth, which they hoped would allow it to be lifted into the air. It had to be precise to make sure the load would be balanced perfectly. Otherwise it would shift and pitch, bringing the two aircrafts down towards the ocean (a scenario made more likely by the constancy of the storm), endangering yet more lives. If the second helicopter did not perform this task successfully, they could only rely on the *Fingal*, the lighthouse boat that was on its way from Oban, to attempt to save the pilot and the injured keeper. With the fury of the storm that was blowing, this seemed an unlikely prospect. Not only would it take much longer but the boat was unlikely to be able to land and bring the two men off the rock. As they saw the second helicopter approaching Skerryvore, they could feel their hearts tolling, their mouths becoming dry, the wind moaning and whistling all around them. They wondered whether what they had done might succeed.

And then the miracle happened – Gordon and Ian among those who watched the rescue helicopter raise the first broken machine from the helipad. It happened slowly, carefully, but definitely, a wondrous levitation above rock and water in the shadow of the tower. The two men watched as the second helicopter carried its

Skerryvore Lighthouse, Argyll & Bute A Listed
A helicopter hovers above the lighthouse in 1984. The helipad also served as an exercise yard during calm days, with keepers grateful for the additional breathing space. Before 1972, when this was built, supplies were delivered to the old and rusting jetty.
HES Canmore SC580018

Rubha Reidh Lighthouse, Highland B Listed

The long and winding road that leads to Rubha Reidh is still a difficult and twisting way to travel. Nowadays the major obstacle to reaching this destination is the white fleece of sheep. Before the road was built, it was the often thunderous white crests of waves.

HES Canmore DP212466, HES 008-000-012-746-R

wounded companion in the web of rope that Gordon had fashioned for it, heading across to the airport in Tiree. A little while later and it was back on Skerryvore, taking the pilot of the other helicopter and the injured man with them, the latter on his way at last to hospital. The pair breathed again, delighted that they had completed a task for which they later received a Letter of Commendation from Ferranti, the company that supplied the helicopter. They might have been conscious that throughout these hours the speed of their pulses resembled the wingbeats of the seabirds that so often surrounded the tower in which they worked.

All lighthouses are miracles of construction. I am conscious of that fact each time I visit places like Rubha Reidh or the Butt of Lewis. It is so easy to gain a false perception of these buildings nowadays, believing their locations have always been simple and easy to reach.

This is because a road now winds its way towards both towers. In Rubha Reidh's case, one has to pass through moor and heather-grazing sheep, across an unstable bridge or two, to reach the 'smooth point' on which the building stands. Approaching the Butt of Lewis, there is a drive over the sweep and sway of lazy-beds till your destination is at hand. As Chris Barratt,[3] the retained lightkeeper at Rubha Reidh (as well as being the 'on call' keeper for other lights, including those on Skye), explained while she stood on the gallery and pointed to a short track that veered off the main route to the lighthouse, the narrow, tarred road that brought the two of us here is a comparatively recent innovation.

'That's where supplies used to arrive before the road was created. The small bay there was where they came ashore.'

I nod, familiar with a similar scenario. The supplies for the Butt of Lewis lighthouse had once arrived in Stoth, a sandy bay a few hundred yards away from the tower. They heaved and hoisted their requirements

3 In recent years, there have been an increasing percentage of female lightkeepers in the service. Looking after several lighthouses both in the north-west Highlands and Skye, Chris is just one of their number.

either up the low cliff that provided a little shelter from the waves or along the concrete slipway at the beach's end, hauling across dips and rises within that landscape. Among the deliveries there would have been air-tanks for the foghorn, perhaps colza oil to fuel the lamp, together with food and other supplies. (Water would not have been brought that way. Instead, it was taken to the tower courtesy of a donkey and cart, carried from a well in the village of Lionel a few miles away.) There would have been moments, too, when visiting notables such as the Commissioners hovered in the air between ship and shore, standing on a 'button', a narrow circle of wood, sent to check that all was well with those who tended the light.

It was not a trouble-free arrangement. A ship carrying goods and equipment was wrecked upon the rocks in the 1860s as it fought its way into the bay – the bricks that were part of its cargo still sometimes found, broken and shattered, in the sand. There were further problems after deliveries had taken place – even before the lighthouse was complete. Only one man among the specialised workforce was capable of creating the 168 steps of the spiral staircase which I clambered up as a child to see my native district from that high and mighty perspective. During its construction, he went on strike, only returning to work when he obtained an extra penny per day in payment for his skills.

This was of course far from the only lighthouse to overcome complications and become a fixture on the Scottish landscape. The lighthouse of Skerryvore, which stands some 48m high on the rocks near Tiree, dwarfs the tower at the Butt of Lewis not only in height, but also in the scale of difficulties in the building process. As someone who has family connections with both islands, I am all too conscious that there were a number of reasons why those from the island in the Inner Hebrides would, even more than their counterparts further north, have distrusted those who planned to build a lighthouse near their coast.

I was reminded of this a few years ago while visiting the white-walled cottage that was my maternal grandparents' home in Balemartine on the west coast of Tiree. A short distance away, my grandson sifted sand with his plastic spade, finding shells, a fragment from a willow-pattern plate, and sea glass, green, brown and clear, long rubbed smooth by the movement of waves. These are by no means the only

items that man and Atlantic have deposited here over the years. Examine a wooden strainer employed to mark the corner post of a crofter's fence and you will often find it is a piece of driftwood, a gift of the tide washed into Scarinish or Crossapol. Step inside that crofter's home and you will sometimes discover that the inside walls are tea-chests or the remnants of old wooden fish-boxes, occasionally delivered to these shores by the same means. Look at the roof of my grandparents' home and you may find that, unlike the thatched cottages that were part of the traditional black houses found in, say, much of the rest of the Hebrides, it consists of canvas, part of the sail of a boat that had been wrecked nearby. Smooth and black, it was coated with either the dark residue of kelp, harvested from the shore here in the bitter, unrelenting labours that took place in the eighteenth and nineteenth century or, in later years, tar or bitumen. In short, the white expanses of Tiree's beaches, nowadays often haunted by surfers eager to launch themselves on waves that stand taller than the low level island they strike, were once the domain of those who hoped to salvage something that could be useful in their lives. This happened here more often than in the north of Lewis, where trading ships passed less frequently on their way to and from the American coast. At one time, the kindness of the waves might even extend to the clothes the islanders wore. Thomas, Chief Clerk of the Board of Trade in London, was sent to investigate the conduct of local officials with regard to wrecks in the islands of North Uist and Barra. He made the following observation in a private letter in 1866, one that could have been written, too, of the inhabitants of other islands and coastal areas throughout Scotland:

For clothing the women seem to wear all sorts of odd things. It was a matter of wonder to me at first, where they got their clothes from. They do not appear to wear as a rule clothes of home manufacture or native wool but to have a selection from a most marvellous miscellaneous collection of old clothes. In fact, among the women of the villages in Barra, you would see specimens, very faded, ragged and worn out it is true, but still specimens of costume that would correspond with any costume from Queen Anne's time downward. The only conclusion I come to is that they get clothes from wrecks and that they obtain the fashions of almost all nations.

He goes onto conclude:

> In the six months ending June 1866 nearly £300,000 worth of property have been washed ashore off the islands on the west coast of Scotland. The islanders look upon this as the special dispensation of a wise providence.

In these short sentences, Gray manages to sum up two different attitudes to the loss of ships on these shores. There is the view of many of those who lived on the coast over the centuries, that the sinking of a vessel in close vicinity was a boon to them and their community, that the loss of human life was an unfortunate accompaniment to a moment of beneficence and grace. There was even the sense

Taigh Fionaghala, Scarinish, Tiree c1898
Even today Tiree has more houses built in the traditional style than any other Scottish island. A few are still thatched. However, in terms of comfort they bear little resemblance to those around at the end of the nineteenth century.
HES Canmore (Erskine Beveridge Collection) SC743220

among some that if you tried to save an individual from drowning, you were putting your own life in peril. After cheating the storm-gods of a potential victim, your own existence would be at risk. This was possibly one reason why survivors of a sinking were sometimes treated with great ruthlessness by those on shore. However, there were other reasons. Once upon a time, dark forces such as the Vikings sailed in the direction of Scotland's shorelines. In later centuries, it might be the coming of the press-gang. No doubt, too, it was often the case that those who sought to defend their sons and daughters, brothers and sisters, from these outrages and intrusions would be raped or killed and their winter stores stripped of their meagre food supplies. In this historical context (and in spite of some of the advantages that came with dwelling by the coast), it is easy to understand why people living near the shoreline – whether they lived on the west or east coast of these islands – would be more than a little wary of new arrivals. Those who travelled in our direction from the ocean had little compassion or care for the settled ones there. No doubt there were times when that lack of feeling or sympathy would be reciprocated.

Whether intentionally or not, however, in his letter Gray also reveals his priorities as a Board of Trade

official. His sole concern is the loss of property. This is despite the fact that, over the previous twenty years or so, many lives had come to an end off the islands of the west coast of Scotland. As can be seen in Allan F Murray's book *The Wreck of the Annie Jane*, over 300 passengers and crew were drowned in a single instance when the voyage of a ship of that name came to an end off Vatersay in the Western Isles in 1853. While this might be an extreme example, it is not the only one. To Thomas Gray and his likes, however, it is not the death of men, women and passengers that really matters. Instead, his concern is about the cargo these ships carried, the wind and wavefall that brought real and tangible benefits to the quality of life experienced by residents of Tiree, Barra, Vatersay, Coll, …

Yet it is not only this attitude, common among businessmen at that time, that may well have made the people of Tiree distrust those who planned to build the lighthouse at Skerryvore. There would have been the sense that prejudice from the outside world – and the mainland of Scotland specifically – had washed into their shores. This time it was a group of Lowlanders who regarded them with ill-disguised scorn, seeing them as unfit for employment. This was exemplified in Alan Stevenson's[4] own words and attitudes. He employed only a few islanders while working on the lighthouse, not trusting them for the task because of their 'incapacity' and 'excessive indolence', as well as the undoubted fact that there were few skilled tradesmen, especially stonemasons, in their midst. There may also have been a reluctance to assist Stevenson and his workforce, perhaps in part a response to a task that would undoubtedly have a negative effect on the future welfare of the islanders, preventing precious cargos from being washed onto their shore. There would also likely have been understandable envy on their part when they saw the sturdy strong walls of the lightkeepers' stores at Hynish – a place where I stayed on two occasions when I visited the island. Above these in the Upper Square are the quarters of the lightkeepers, the gardens walled to prevent the whip of salt, sea and sand from

Hynish Shore Station, Tiree, Argyll & Bute A Listed
Upper Square in Hynish now provides homes for island families. At one time it was occupied by lightkeepers who relayed messages to their counterparts by means of the nearby Signal Tower.
HES SC743220, DP244578

devastating and destroying the vegetables planted within. The walls have stood up well to the weather, but perhaps the ghosts of those islanders would have let slip a rueful laugh when they saw the condition of the dock they overlook. Its length and depth is silted and blocked with sand, for all Stevenson's plans to flush it clean with water from a reservoir a short distance away. The dock was a forlorn attempt to supply Tiree with one resource it still lacks today – a natural harbour, the reason why its shore station[5] was eventually transferred to Erraid west of Mull in Argyll (the harbour, as well as other lighthouse buildings, has been restored by the Hebridean Trust over the past few decades). It was this work, encompassing all these different developments, that began in 1837. At first, locally quarried grey gneiss was used in the labour. However, this was a difficult material to work. Later, quarrying was switched to Camas Tuath on the Ross of Mull where the pink granite was easier to shape. The different shades of these stones are in evidence in the buildings around Hynish. And all this came complete with its own round tower: one similar to the Signal Tower in Arbroath though standing at a short distance from the harbour, flagging up and signalling information to the men stationed in Skerryvore. (This included news of whether their wives had given birth to a boy or girl: a set of short trousers was rolled out in the former case, a skirt in the latter.)

We can only imagine the feelings of the average Tirisdeach, the term used for a native of Tiree, who would have looked out from their traditional houses as these dramatic new structures arose on the edge of their island. And Alan Stevenson, for one, was not unaware of the contrasts. Coming close to revelling in them, he noted that:

> the desolation and misery of the surrounding hamlets of Tyree seemed to enhance the

4 Alan Stevenson was the second generation of Stevensons to work as an engineer on Scotland's lighthouses. As he says in his 1848 publication *Account of the Skerryvore Lighthouse*, 'I must acknowledge my many and great obligations to my Father … of whose experience, as the Architect of no fewer than twenty-five Lighthouses, including that of the Bell Rock, I had the full benefit during the erection of the Skerryvore Lighthouse.'

5 Lighthouses on rocks or remote islands such as Flannan Isles, Skerryvore and Bell Rock had shore stations for lightkeepers and their families. Others – like the Butt of Lewis, Cape Wrath, Kinnaird Head and so on – did not require them as the families stayed near the light.

satisfaction of looking on our small colony, where about 150 souls were collected in a neat quadrangle of cleanly houses, conspicuous by their chimneys and windows amongst the hovels of the poor Hebrideans.

Yet there was more indeed than all of that. During the years the lighthouse was being built, the people of Tiree were already experiencing major problems, its rising population crammed into smaller and smaller segments of land. In around 1750, there were 1,509 people living on the island (compared to around 650 today); in 1801, a total of 2,776. By 1841, a year when Stevenson's workforce was engaged in building the lighthouse, there were 4,900 individuals in Hynish's 'surrounding hamlets', the majority, as their landlord the Duke of Argyll (who in fact laid the foundation stone of Skerryvore lighthouse) noted in the 1883 publication *Crofts and Farms in the Hebrides*, 'a vast semi-pauper population'. This meant that many relied on a basic diet of potatoes, in Stevenson's view an essential element in the 'incapacity' and 'excessive indolence' the people displayed. This was intensified later in 1846 when this crop, too, failed, causing hunger and starvation. This situation also led to the cruel evictions that had started to take place in both Tiree and its near neighbour the Ross of Mull during this time, with the Duke of Argyll among others 'encouraging' tenants to leave his estate for locations like the Scottish mainland and Canada rather than providing them with charity and support to stay at home. While the people there may not have suffered the brutality experienced by those who were the victims of this process in, say, Sutherland or the islands of South Uist or Barra, members of around 40 households were evicted directly by the Duke. His tenants on Tiree must also have been acutely aware of a pattern of similar incidents in the neighbouring isle of Mull, where the walls of villages where people once lived still stand – and crumble – today. In short, there were many reasons for the 'listless, dispirited and squalid look of the poor Celts' that – in his own words – surrounded young Alan Stevenson at that time.

The islanders watched, however, the activity occurring on their horizon, 10 nautical miles to the south-west. Much of the work was based on Alan Stevenson's observation and knowledge of the island where they lived. With the strength of the waves as they powered in from the Atlantic, he began to realise that the base of the lighthouse had to be solid stone, especially as the hardness of the Lewisian gneiss below would not allow the building of foundations. As a result of this, a team of 80 stonemasons worked throughout the chill of winter in Hynish, giving shape to over 4,300 blocks that could be transported to the rock and set in position without any changes or adjustment. In Gourock, a six-legged wooden barracks was created and brought to the rock around midsummer 1838. This, in principle, would allow 40 men to sleep on the rock. For all that 21 men sweated over the construction of this building for 16 hours a day, five days a week, it proved no match for a Tiree gale. On 3 November, no doubt much to the delight of any cynics who wanted their dark prophecies fulfilled, the waves were transformed into a magician's cloth and, as they had done so often in history, swept it completely away.

Lesser men might have shaken their heads and sailed from Tiree's shore, never to return. It is a mark of Alan Stevenson's courage and endurance that he did not, despite the fact that progress was slow the following year, with cranes, tools and materials being stolen by the ocean. Rough seas frequently deprived the workers of food and fuel. The building of a second, stronger barracks for the men, some 60 foot (18m) in height and often rocked and penetrated by the ocean, was completed on 3 September. Using almost 300 charges of gunpowder, they also removed over 200 tons of rock, leaving in the middle of this broken, fractured surface, an impressive circular floor, 42 feet in diameter, as smooth as – that rarity in the waters around the Inner Hebrides – a calm and waveless sea. It was on this base they planned to build the entire structure of the lighthouse.

Miraculously, when they sailed out there the following year in 1840, they found the barracks had withstood the whirl of the winter's winds, a little battered and bruised by the trials of that season, but essentially in one piece. This must have energised the workers who returned there. They embarked on the task to build the tower. By the end of the season, over 8 foot (2m) was in its place, 85 blocks laid in a day. It set a precedent for the following years. By July 1842, the final stone was added to the 97th course. The masonry of the tower was now 137 feet 11 inches (42m) in height, and it contained 58,580 cubic feet (1,659 cubic metres) of material of about 4,308 tons. Through August and September, the lantern arrived in

Skerryvore Lighthouse

With its granite walls, Skerryvore is regarded by many as one of Scotland's most outstanding and graceful lighthouses, without the paint that colours the surface of many. Its optical apparatus also outshone its rivals, being designed by Alan Stevenson in collaboration with French engineer, Augustin Fresnel.

Ian Cowe

sections and was assembled. Less than two years later, in February 1844, the people of Tiree looked out to see a strange new light. Transforming their surroundings, it added a new gleam to the star-speckled sky that stretched above the shores of their islands, warning approaching vessels of the rocks that were nearby.

It must surely have impressed them. It is a tower that – as a few people who have visited there have told me – seems to defy gravity, looking as if, even on a still, calm day, it is just about to topple and fall upon a man's insignificant height. It also has an astonishing symmetry in terms of its outline, with its height of 156ft (48m), the diameter of 42ft (13m) at the base tapering to 16ft (5m) at the top. And then there is the rosy shade of the stone from which it is built, quarried from the Ross of Mull. Even for a people who had Tiree's beaches in their eyeline, with its golden swathe of sand, Skerryvore possessed a remarkable grace and beauty, one which is still appreciated today.

There is more even than that. Yet another remarkable aspect about the construction of Skerryvore is that Alan Stevenson accomplished all this without the loss of a single life. This suggests a respect and regard for human life that seemed utterly absent in those who held sway in the islands, especially through the next few years of the potato famine and the bitterness of the Clearances that followed. For all that Stevenson and his workforce had sometimes regarded them with contempt, the islanders could see that a concern for others lay at the base of his working practices.

In the years after the Stevensons built lighthouses around our coast many men from islands like Tiree applied for posts with the Northern Lighthouse Board. Given Stevenson's attitude to the 'listless dispirited' population who surrounded him, there is more than a little irony in this. The Northern Lighthouse Board came to employ those from rural areas, often islands, particularly those individuals who possessed knowledge of the sea and all its ways, more often than those who originated in cities like Edinburgh or Glasgow. As well as being aware of the relentless and destructive nature of the ocean, they were deemed to be better at coping with isolation, able to while away their hours in pursuit of some craft rather than feeling restless and confined within the tower. This was why men like Alex Macleod from the Isle of Lewis, who was the first principal lightkeeper Ian Duff saw when arriving in Skerryvore, could be found spending their working lives cut off from the wider world. Or indeed men like Donald MacDonald from Assynt in the north-west Highlands, who was eulogised in a moving and touching tribute by the *Daily Mail* columnist John Macleod. An individual who served on Ailsa Craig, Fair Isle South, Ardnamurchan and Skerryvore, Donald was 'comfortable with silence' even in his early twenties when he began this employment, able to endure 'the limited conversation; the much older men, and the dull food, largely from tins and packets'. This was clearly before the time some lightkeepers managed to persuade the Northern Lighthouse Board to invest in a deep freeze for the bottom floor.

And it is possible that the existence of the lighthouse did more than that. Tiree – along with the community of Sandness in Shetland – is one of two places I have visited where residents claim to have produced more ship captains than any other part of Scotland. Whether this abundance of captains can be laid directly at the feet of Skerryvore may be a matter of speculation, but even today there are examples of local islanders stepping into this role. One notable case is Eric Smith from the village of Barvas in Lewis, someone I have known for many years, having been a close friend and contemporary of his late brother Angus. A slight figure with a shy, quiet smile, he has a similar exactness in his speech as he must do on the bridge of the *Pole Star* where he works, ensuring that his vessel reaches the quayside in as precise and trouble-free a manner as possible. There is a calmness about him that – I imagine – merits and justifies respect on the part of others.

The Northern Lighthouse Board was not where he began his career. Instead, like several men I recall from my home district in my youth, he worked deep sea in the Merchant Navy. Some years later, he saw an advert in the *Press and Journal* for a temporary contract working on the Northern Lighthouse Board boat the *Pole Star*. He applied, and after a short conversation with the Marine Superintendent, obtained the post. The contract rolled on … and on … and on. Initially, he spent eight weeks on, four weeks off the boat. Later, in 1988, this altered to four weeks on, four weeks off. Most of the time he was with the *Pole Star*, the vessel tied up at its home port of Stromness, the base for duties across Orkney, Shetland, the north coast of Scotland and the north-west coast of Scotland including Skye,

Lewis and Harris and the Flannan Isles during much of this period. The boat was fitted with a helipad, like its counterpart, the *Fingal*, in the early eighties, and its tasks included the maintenance of the navigation buoys around Scotland's coastline, lifting them carefully out of the water and ensuring they were working properly. (At one time, as Peddie's photographs show, the men from these vessels used to clamber on the buoys, ensuring that all was in order as they rocked perilously back and forth.) In addition, they replenished the stores on lighthouses, using both the helicopter and ships' boats. At that time, too, they provided occasional relief for Bell Rock – the one that, together with Skerryvore, Eric finds the most impressive of Scotland's lighthouses. 'It's a toss-up between them. I always think it astonishing the way they managed to build Bell Rock lighthouse at the time it was created. Especially with the way the rock on which it stands is frequently washed over by waves.'

After a while, he moved onto a full-time contract, becoming Second Mate of the *Pole Star* in 1988. In 1991, he shifted to Oban, becoming second mate of the *Fingal*, covering the coastline from Skye and the southern end of the Western Isles to the Solway Firth, including the Isle of Man. When I spoke to him one night, almost 20 years later, the vessel was anchored outside Turnberry, the lights of Donald Trump's hotel clearly seen from the bridge. Eric also reflected on the third Northern Lighthouse Board vessel, the *Pharos*, which during the 1980s sailed out of what was then the Board's key base, Granton near Edinburgh, to cover the east coast of Scotland from the Borders to Duncansby Head in Caithness. Though it lacked a helideck at that time, its duties were identical to the *Pole Star* and *Fingal* – with one exception. Both then and now it ferried the Commissioners on their annual voyage inspecting the lighthouses on Scotland's shores.

'They can go anywhere. The whole thing's not as grand as it used to be in the days when Peddie took his photos,' he declared, 'But it's still really important.'

During his long career, Eric has served – on occasion – on all three vessels. His most dramatic moment came on the *Pharos*, returning to Montrose after a visit to an oilrig in the North Sea. It was a task they were employed to do by the Department of Energy, ensuring that all the proper safety measures were in place, that the oilrigs' lights could be seen, their navigation aids all in order.

NLV *Pharos* at Bell Rock Lighthouse

The Northern Lighthouse Board vessel the *Pharos* waits at
Bell Rock with its helipad in action.

Sean Boyce

But it was the voyage home on the last night of the
inspection that has really stayed in Eric's mind. He was
asleep at the time, unaware that the sea was crinkling
below him, the wind beginning to lift and blow. First
there was one knock, followed by another. His eyes
shot open. A moment or two later he was out on the
bridge, watching a storm cut loose and the *Pharos*
lurching from side to side as the waves heaved it to and
fro, descending into the maelstrom …

'One second, we were rising on a swell and the next
we were down in the depths of a hole, plummeting

into the depths. We watched the weight of waves
breaking over the bridge, leaving it damaged and in
need of repair. Our feet were rocking too, our balance
stolen from us for a moment or two. Everyone's nerves
were frayed by the time we reached the harbour. It was
the worst sailing I've ever been on, but somehow we
made it back.'

Finally, outweighing the rough crossings, there is
the scenery of Scotland's coastline, especially its west
coast. Places like the Cuillins of Skye where on cold
frosty mornings Eric feels he could touch the chilly
magnificence of their peaks if he just stretched out his
hand. And that's not to mention places like Muckle
Flugga lighthouse and the others that stand on both the
mainland of Shetland's jagged edge and the tiny islands
– like Foula and the Out Skerries – that lie around …

Chapter 6

Watchman, What of the Night?

The Lighthouse in Times of War

At the foot of the lighthouse it is dark.

Japanese proverb, quoted in J Long,
Eastern Proverbs and Emblems
Illustrating Old Truths

It's on days when the plane comes into Shetland pitching and rolling that I most appreciate the sight of Sumburgh lighthouse. Its cluster of white buildings seems to almost brush the aircraft's wingtips as it veers towards land, the storm rocking and shaking metal, causing my fellow-passengers and me to clasp our seats, fearing that the pilot might not make contact with the runway, that at best we might have to turn around and go back to Orkney or the mainland, that at worst … My eyes close at the thought. No sooner does it dash through my head than I look out the window and see the lighthouse tower, finding in its presence a gleam of hope that we might return to earth safe and secure.

It is that building, too, I often glance at when the plane comes to a standstill outside the terminal, looking upwards instead of downwards as I might have done a few minutes before touchdown. It stands

Sumburgh Head Lighthouse, Shetland A Listed

As planes sweep into nearby Sumburgh Airport, an aerial view of the lighthouse can often be glimpsed by passengers as they approach land.

HES Canmore DP081345

perched above the cliff-tops at the southern tip of Shetland, sometimes obscured by a veil of rain or mist, at other times, especially after its recent renovation, as bright and sparkling as the very light it contains. Spend a while there on a sunlit day and it is clear why it is such an important landmark for the people of Shetland. Looking north, I can see the villages of Sandwick and Cunningsburgh, the cliffs of Noss with their pitching, veering gannets, the broch at Mousa with its circular structure still intact, a haven for the flocks of storm petrels that nest within its walls. Peering south, I can see an array of skerries and rocks, the outline of Fair Isle. Switch direction and there is the sweep of coastline with all its voes and bays, the Iron Age village of Old Scatness, excavated only in the last five decades, and Jarlshof with its layers of time – from the Iron Age to the Norse era, to a medieval farm. For an instant, it is as if I am back on that plane, taking in all the sights and wonders down below. The flight is more smooth and calm on this occasion as I look out on the backs of puffins, kittiwakes and fulmars as they cross the distances between rock and cliff, wave and nest, and I am able too, to comprehend just how long man has succeeded in eking out an existence here.

As befits its height – 91m above sea-level – long before the building of the lighthouse, Sumburgh was a place of warning. Its title 'Sumburgh' underlines this. It means 'south fortification', a term derived from Norse 'sunn', meaning south and 'burgh' meaning fortified place – the same word as 'broch' (as in Mousa Broch not far away). The remains of the ancient stronghold are still there today – not that I noticed them till I walked down the slope that leads to the lighthouse in the company of an RSPB staff member there, Helen Moncrieff, who stays nearby in the South Mainland of Shetland. For once she was without the company of Casino, the three-legged greyhound with which she is often seen when walking round the community. I note the absence of her dog when she takes me on a short stroll outside the lighthouse gate. 'You don't look quite whole,' I laughed. 'I'm not,' she confessed. 'I love Casino by my side. Don't feel complete without the company.'

She pointed then to a thin ridge of stone that lay just outside the wall around the lighthouse. 'There it is,' she declared, indicating a second time when I failed to see it. 'That line there.'

It took me a moment before I focused on it – a barely visible furrow cut across tussocks of coarse grass. This spine of rock was all that remained of the Iron Age fort that once been on this headland. Such was its vantage point that it may have been from this location that the men from my native Isle of Lewis were spotted as they launched a raid on the South Mainland many centuries ago. According to that tradition, the bodies of the invaders ended up within burial mounds at Scousburgh, the local men having guided and trapped them there. I looked at Helen a shade suspiciously as I recalled that story; her three-legged companion, perhaps the ideal way to round up errant Hebrideans who had travelled in Sumburgh's direction.

This wasn't the only warning that had been issued from Sumburgh over the years. Among the lighthouse buildings there is a large foghorn, which, for all it was officially silenced in 1987, still sounds – with the help and expertise of lighthouse engineer Brian Johnson – from time to time even today. This glimpse of past technology attracts a substantial number of visitors who wish to hear its loud and solemn note. It is also one of the largest of its kind I have seen, bringing to mind the white tapered foghorn that stood on the Butt of Lewis, before the rock below its foundation had been undermined and the structure had to be taken down in 1995. With its bright scarlet shade, the horn reminds me of the bell of a tuba, its deep notes once resounding whenever the keepers saw fit to caution ships that the haar that surrounded them was thick and dangerous, a hazard to either their lives or the

Sumburgh Airport, August 1940

A frontline view caught in the camera of German pilots in the early years of the Second World War.
HES NCAP SC799779

voyages they were set upon. At one time, it could be swirled round to alter the sound's direction, letting the fishermen on either side of the peninsula know that one of Shetland's frequent mists had settled on the landscape, that danger was all around. In one of the buildings near the foghorn, there is a large engine room which was the source of the foghorn's notes. It looks pristine and clear, polished and restored during the renovation of the site a few years before.[1] Brian eases the mechanism that produces the sound with a few drops of oil, listening to it click and ratchet into position, before he runs outside to a white shed where he triggers the noise, unleashing the depth of its drone on all that are gathered nearby, including the seabirds scattering from the cliffs.

There are also elements of a former radar station found among the cluster of buildings on the crest of Sumburgh Head, a reminder of the important role that Shetland played in both the First and Second World Wars. Just as the Strait of Dover was a dangerous stretch of water, enemy shipping and submarines often channelled their way through the North Sea and around Orkney and Shetland to reach the North Atlantic. As a result of this, it was an important place for the Royal Navy and Royal Air Force to patrol, trying to stop the German fleet and others slipping through these waters.

The information boards around the lighthouse tell part of this story, how the radar station at this point was the first of a number that would later come into operation in northern Scotland. In doing this, it has been argued, the existence of the radar station was in breach of the Geneva Convention which – both the Ministry of Shipping and the Northern Lighthouse Board argued – did not allow the building of a military installation within lighthouse grounds,

1 For all its omnipresence later, the foghorn was late coming to Scotland with the first built at St Abb's Head in Berwickshire in only 1876. Imported from America, it was first developed on that continent but its inventor was Scottish emigrant Robert Foulis (1796–1866). He invented his steam-power foghorn with its low-pitched sound after he overheard his daughter playing piano when he was taking a long walk in fog near his home in Saint John, New Brunswick. He was conscious that he could hear her low-pitched notes from farther away than he could the high notes.

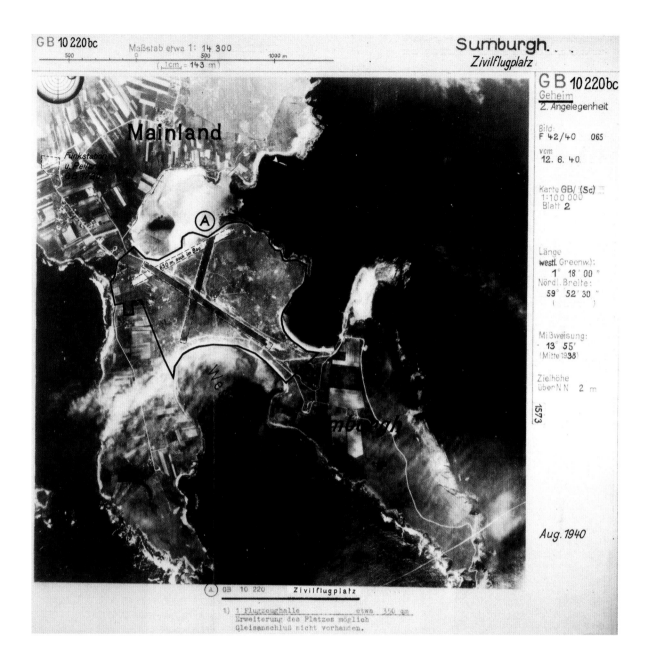

GB 10 220 bc

Maßstab etwa 1: 14 300

(1 cm = 143 m)

Sumburgh.
Zivilflugplatz

GB 10 220 bc
Geheim
2. Angelegenheit

Bild:
F 42/40   065

vom
12. 6. 40.

Karte GB/ (Sc)
1:100 000
Blatt 2

Länge
westl. Greenw.):
1° 18' 00"
Nördl. Breite:
59° 52' 30"

Mißweisung:
- 13° 55'
(Mitte 1938)

Zielhöhe
über NN   2 m

1573

Mainland

Aug. 1940

Ⓐ GB 10 220   Zivilflugplatz

1) 1 Flugzeughalle   etwa 350 qm
Erweiterung des Platzes möglich
Gleisanschluß nicht vorhanden.

especially for belligerent purposes. They underlined this by pointing out that lighthouses were not legitimate military targets. An Admiralty letter written on 17 December 1939 countered this by pointing out that, in their view, the Convention only stated that they should not be used for 'overtly military purposes'.

Regardless of such niceties, Sumburgh Head Admiralty Experimental Station 1 was already in operation by this time. Building began in autumn

1939 and it was completed by December of that year when the first watch started. Their whole approach was unconventional in other ways. For all that the station was manned by the Navy and protected by an army guard, the officers who worked there were not the usual men involved in military operations, but a group of university professionals who were normally employed in Greenland and an Arctic expedition in Baffin Island. Their commanding officer Richard

Feachem was a 25-year old naval sub-lieutenant when he arrived at Sumburgh Head, having graduated with an archaeological degree two years earlier. He later went on to develop expertise in his chosen subject, writing fully and extensively on Pictish hillforts and similar subject matter in his career after the war. Another officer, George Clifford Evans, was a plant physiologist. He later became President of the British Ecological Society between the years 1975 and 1976 and Chairman of the British Photobiological Society between 1979 and 1981. In addition, this unlikely war-veteran was a fellow and Bursar of St John's College, Cambridge, and author of the textbook *The Quantitative Analysis of Plant Growth*. Given the bare landscape of Shetland and its lack of sunlight during the winter months, it is safe to assume that he did not pursue two of his later specialities while stationed in Sumburgh – exploring sunflecks and light interception in forest understories.

Yet these men and their colleagues may have played a major role in the outcome of the Second World War, doing much to frustrate a surprise German air raid which took place in the evening of 8 April 1940. This was the night when around 60 Luftwaffe planes took off from various bases in Germany. Their target was Scapa Flow in Orkney, where the entire British Home Fleet was at anchor, having returned in March to a stretch of water that would be close to the site of the future Churchill Barriers. Their construction would begin the following month, set in place for the protection of the British fleet following the sinking of the *Royal Oak* by a U-boat in these waters the previous October. By September 1944, the barriers would be complete.

That day in April 1940 was one when those stationed in Sumburgh lighthouse were probably at their highest state of vigilance. The same date was the beginning of Operation Wilfred, when the Royal Navy was starting to mine the Norwegian Corridor, the stretch of water between Norway's mainland and its offshore islands. This was to prevent Germany from importing the iron ore required to manufacture steel for tanks, ships and aircraft by forcing the vessels that brought this supply into open waters. It was partly in response to this possibility that the Germans began to build up their troops and shipping in Baltic ports such as Rostock, Stettin and Swinemünde. The activity was a sign that a Nazi invasion of Denmark and Norway was being planned

– an event that occurred the following day, 9 April. The attempt to destroy the British Home Fleet in Scapa Flow was all part of the strategy to ensure that this could be done swiftly and efficiently.

It was the man who would one day become an important ecologist, Sub-lieutenant George Clifford Evans, who was in charge that evening. Some 25 minutes before the attack happened, he was able to let the commanding officer in Lyness on the east coast of the island of Hoy in Orkney know that planes were flying in their direction, allowing the artillery time to prepare for the arrival of the Luftwaffe. After he had done so, he stepped out to watch the flash of heavy guns, the barrage of bullets and bombs that streamed across and streaked the night sky, imagining the dip and swirl of the planes above the waters of the Flow and the forces seeking to defend the ships below. He could hear the rattle and clash too, disturbed by its clamour just like those in Lerwick, some 125 miles away from the fighting, who also heard its echo in the distance. It was said to be 'the longest continuous sound' ever before heard throughout the length and breadth of the British Isles, the noise prolonged, perhaps, by the nerves and fears of those who listened to it many miles from its source.

But, for all its uproar, the raid was unsuccessful; the early warning provided by the Sumburgh lighthouse radar team helped to prevent the destruction of the fleet, part of the effort to ensure the war was less likely to be lost, especially at this early stage in the conflict. George Clifford Evans noted later that 'no serious damage had been done' to Britain's war-effort that day, adding that he had informed the crew of men around him 'that if the station never made any other contribution to the war we had already justified the entire enterprise'.

It was not the only time that Sumburgh was touched by war. As early as April 1939, the keepers there would have been preparing for the likelihood of conflict. A letter inscribed with the words 'Top Secret' would have arrived both for them and others around the coast of Scotland. It included a second sealed envelope which they were informed they should only open if they received a telegram with the words 'Institute Phase 1A'. Within it was held a note with the instruction 'Extinguish your light now'. Unlike the First World War, however, where the coastline became a dark, hazard-filled experience

Scapa Flow, Orkney, April 1940

Hoy, Flotta, South Ronaldsay, Orkney mainland and the waters of
Scapa Flow – caught in the eyeline of Luftwaffe pilots in April 1940.
HES NCAP SC449543

for the vessels that wound their way around it, the
lights were not turned off by default.[2] Instead they
were controlled by the Admiralty who communicated
with keepers by radio and dictated the hours they were
displayed. On the east coast of Scotland, they were
switched off most of the time.

There may have been other strategies. My relative
Angus Smith told me that, during the Second World
War, the RAF used to bring a trailer carrying a light
to a half-circle of road outside his home in the village
of North Dell. For whatever purpose, this would
sometimes be switched on, its beam rotating in the
darkness from this location. It is unclear whether the
character of this light was designed to be confused
with the one, say, on Cape Wrath or the Butt of

Lewis a few miles north. It might even have been a
searchlight they were testing, far from the country's
industrial heartlands.

The only exception to Admiralty control was when
an air-raid signal swirled and sounded across the local
area, the response of the lightkeepers on duty to turn
off the light taking precedence in these situations.
There was one anomaly – a lighthouse left in complete
darkness for many of the war years, and indeed some
50 years afterwards. The Monach Isles, a light which
I used to see frequently when I lived and worked in
Benbecula, was switched off during the conflict. It
was abandoned in September 1942 when there were
problems reaching the keeper stationed there with
supplies and sustenance. Frequently, the provisions,
after lying for weeks in Bayhead, North Uist, were
deemed to be 'useless' by the time they reached the
men stationed there.

Those in Orkney and Shetland had different
problems. After the fall of Norway, these islands were
considered likely to be invaded by German troops.
If this ever occurred, the keepers at Sumburgh Head
were given special instructions on how to react. They
were told they should not destroy the light entirely
but take measures instead to render it 'temporarily

2 During the First World War, the lights could be turned on at
the request of the Admiralty. This was not always easy to achieve,
however – in 1915 the British HMS *Argyll* was wrecked at Bell Rock
after the message to turn on the light failed to reach the keepers.
Fortunately, the ship's crew survived this incident.

out of action'. They were to bury or conceal any lamp or its parts, waste all the oil they possessed and – if time allowed – remove all the clockwork machinery that enabled the lens to rotate. Thankfully this was a situation that never arose.

As in many of the lighthouses throughout Scotland, the men stationed in Sumburgh to tend the light were also likely to have been engaged in looking out for signs of the conflict that had engulfed them, especially in the early years of the war. As they stepped out on the gallery, below the cupola of the light, the evidence would have been all around them – in the occasional glimpse of a U-boat, its periscope peering above the surface of the water, the awareness that mines were being laid in their vicinity, the sound of depth charges shuddering through lighthouse walls as destroyers and frigates fired them, seeking to protect and preserve the convoys they were charged to keep safe. There

Kinnaird Head Lighthouse, Fraserburgh, 1 August 1939
The town of Fraserburgh edging into the headland it occupies. Kinnaird Head, along with its Wine Tower (bottom left), is among the best preserved of the 'nine castles of the knuckle' on Scotland's north-eastern coast.
HES Canmore (Aerofilms Collection) SC1258311

would have been wreckage too, the flotsam of empty lifeboats, the final remnants of a vessel that had gone down. In the book *Archie's Lights: The Life and Times of a Scottish Lighthouse Keeper*, Archie MacEachern tells of how they often saw animals floating on the waters around Dubh Artach in the Inner Hebrides where he was stationed during the Second World War. Mainly this was livestock – sheep, cattle, horses, even a hen which was part of a cargo bound from Canada. One day he looked out of the lighthouse window to see a large bloated elephant, accompanied by two mules and various other corpses floating past. He arrived at the conclusion that: 'these must have come from a consignment of circus animals being shipped to America'.

There are many other dramas recounted in Archie's rich and rewarding book, put together by his daughter Anne. He tells of how one day a four-engined German Focke-Wulf circled the lighthouse at Dubh Artach for around 15 minutes. The keepers cowered at the doorway, prepared to leap into the waters if a bomb was dropped. Nothing happened. Instead, the plane flew away in the direction of Skerryvore to the north. It dropped six bombs there, none making a direct hit on the lighthouse or the rock on which it stood. They exploded in the sea with only one blast having any effect on the building, breaking the lantern and disabling its light. This was easily fixed after the lightkeepers fitted emergency storm panes and repaired the damage, the signal once again appearing the following night.

As dawn broke during another nightwatch at the lighthouse, Archie observed, too, a British submarine sink a German U-boat out on the horizon from Dubh Artach. On another occasion the keepers saw seven lifeboats drift past the tower, full of huddled figures, some – as far as they could tell – just as likely to be dead as alive. At this point, unable to maintain the neutrality or radio silence that was required of them in wartime when conflict was occurring nearby, they called for help. The response changed little. It was two days before a frigate arrived, too late to save any of those on board these boats.

Other Scottish lighthouses were also sometimes the target of German attacks during the Second World War. This altered the attitude of many people who lived near lighthouse towers, seeing them at that time as less of a solace than a threat. Instead of viewing them as the means to guide fishing boats to the safety of their ports, they now perceived them as waymarks for Germans fighters and bombers; the people of Fraserburgh objecting when, for instance, the Admiralty instructed the lightkeepers at Kinnaird Head to display their light for five minutes every hour and half-hour. There was also an issue with the shade of certain towers, with citizens pointing fingers in their direction and accusing them of guiding enemy attacks to their locality with the limewash that frequently coloured their outside walls. It was this that led the Northern Lighthouse Board to stop this practice

during the war-years, with Scurdie Ness lighthouse outside Montrose even being painted black to avoid the attentions of the enemy.

Yet, for all that measures like this were taken, still they came …

Around 30 attacks by German planes took place on Scottish lighthouses during the Second World War. They machine-gunned lighthouses throughout the length of the country – from Duncansby in Caithness to Barns Ness in East Lothian. Even the Butt of Lewis lighthouse was peppered with bullets on 16 November 1940, the sole 'air raid' experienced by my native island during the Second World War. The same was true at Holborn Head, also in Caithness, Stroma between the Scottish mainland and Orkney, and Auskerry in Orkney, where a crater can be found from one of two bombs dropped on the lighthouse in 1941. The other unexploded bomb has never been discovered. After this incident, however, the lighthouse was supplied with two anti-aircraft Hotchkiss guns, one to the south and the other to the north of the lighthouse buildings, to be manned by the lightkeepers.[3]

Keepers at Rattray Head, Aberdeenshire, endured their proximity when on 20 September 1941 an enemy plane circled the lighthouse, dropping three bombs in their vicinity, including one which did not explode. No one was injured. For all that the lantern was machine-gunned, the damage had no serious effect on the light. Bell Rock was machine-gunned several times, with a bomb dropping nearby and exploding on 1 April 1941, a short distance away from the tower. Again, the keepers were fortunate. There were no lives lost and little more than a few panes of glass shattered. The lens at that time, now on display at the Signal Tower in Arbroath, was also studded by bullets. A temporary light had to be rigged for a time.

It was, of course, not only lighthouses that were targeted. During nights when there was a 'bomber's moon', when the cities, towns and villages were in black-out but the land was clear in the moonlight, any building that cast its shadow on ground or water was a potential target. Fraserburgh was attacked during the early years of the war on 16 July 1940, with three bombs injuring 36 people. Another more serious attack occurred on 5 November of that year

3 These frequently jammed, as those stationed on the Butt of Lewis discovered the one time they were visited by German aircraft.

when 34 people were killed, with 52 other casualties. The Kinnaird Head lighthouse was not the main target in these or other raids or similar incidents. These were undoubtedly the Consolidated Pneumatic Toolworks, which operated as a munitions factory, and Maconochie's Kinnaird Head Works nearby, which provided tinned rations for the overseas troops fighting for the Allied cause. It was during a raid on the latter in February 1941 that damage was caused to some of the rooms and windows, including a bullet which is still to this day lodged in one of Kinnaird Head lighthouse's hyper-radial lenses.

Yet, for all that Fraserburgh was attacked with an intensity that gave it – at one time – the nickname of Little London, there is little doubt that in the first years of the war it was in the Northern Isles, from the Pentland Skerries north to Unst, that the conflict seemed most bizarre and surreal. This was especially true when one considered much of the surrounding landscape. There was no heavy industry, only the grazing sheep on the moorland or green fields, the cattle sheltering beside moss-covered walls when wind and rain made both humans and animals shiver, the sea lapping on the jagged coastline. Among all that, there were many strange contrasts and contradictions. They included the fact that, on 13 November 1939, one of the earliest German bombs to fall on British soil exploded at Sullom in Shetland. Aimed at the vessels docked there, said to be two cruisers, HMS *Cardiff* and HMS *Coventry*, a number of cargo ships and nine flying boats, the bombs instead struck the shoreline and landed in a peat-bog, churning up the ground. In June 1941, the Yell post office was targeted with one man, Daniel Spence, being wounded and several others in the tiny village of Gutcher having a fortunate escape. On 22 February 1941, the enemy machine-gunned the lighthouse buildings in the Pentland Skerries. Luckily, no real damage was inflicted on either the structures or the keepers, one of whom, Angus Macaulay, had already been subjected to a German attack while stationed at Bell Rock. For all that he must have felt jinxed, no real harm was caused.

This was not true in every case. German planes frequently flew over the islands at low altitude, alarming both cattle and crofters. In 1941 they strafed the island of Grunay – now deserted – lying 10 miles east of the Shetland mainland, attacking the Out Skerries lighthouse shore station that was there. They also dropped a bomb in the same vicinity in 1942,

because – according to the German broadcaster and propagandist William Joyce ('Lord Haw-Haw') – there was an ammunition dump situated within its borders. The latter attack killed Mary Anderson, the only local casualty of the war. It was an event recounted to me by her nephew Peter Johnson, a retired Shetland fisherman. She had been the widow of W L (Willie) Anderson, the boatman to the Skerries lighthouse, who had been involved in the rescue of the Swedish vessel the *Advena* some 30 years before.[4] She was staying in the home of their son John James Anderson, who had succeeded his father in that role. It was while John James was away in their storehouse, collecting potatoes for their Sunday dinner, that the attack on their home occurred. He emerged to find the house destroyed, the door-handle and the debris on the path before him. It is an incident that Peter can recall all these years later. 'My father was standing at the back door of our house, holding my sister in his arms, when he heard the plane. Moments later, when he realised what was happening, he slammed the door closed. When he opened it a little while afterwards, the dust had settled. The bricks of the lighthouse dwelling where his aunt was staying were scattered everywhere.'

For all that Grunay was evacuated a short time later, this was not the only time it was touched by war. On 21 February 1942, a Canadian bomber crashed on the island with its crew of two Canadians and one Englishman on board immediately killed. This was an incident that Peter could remember hearing from inside his home. 'I heard one engine stopping. Then the other one struggling. It touched the ground as it tried to effect a landing. But …'[5]

And then there was that other unlikely centre of wartime conflict, tiny Fair Isle, which lies between the southern tip of Shetland and the northern edge of Orkney, where Archie MacEachern was stationed from 1936 to 1939. During the early spring of his last year of service there, a young German who claimed to be a journalist turned up at Fair Isle North, asking if he could see around the lighthouse. Despite his supposed

---

4 See page 91.
5 Barra Head lighthouse, on the southern end of the Outer Hebrides on the island of Berneray, also narrowly missed being hit by a British Blenheim bomber during the Second World War. However, its arrival – presumably at night – was not noticed till the conflict was over, when someone scaling the cliff-face on which the lighthouse is situated became aware of the wreckage of the plane among the rocks.

Fraserburgh, December 1940

The harbour and *Funkstation* (radio transmitter) at
Fraserburgh – annotated by the Luftwaffe.
HES NCAP SC449530

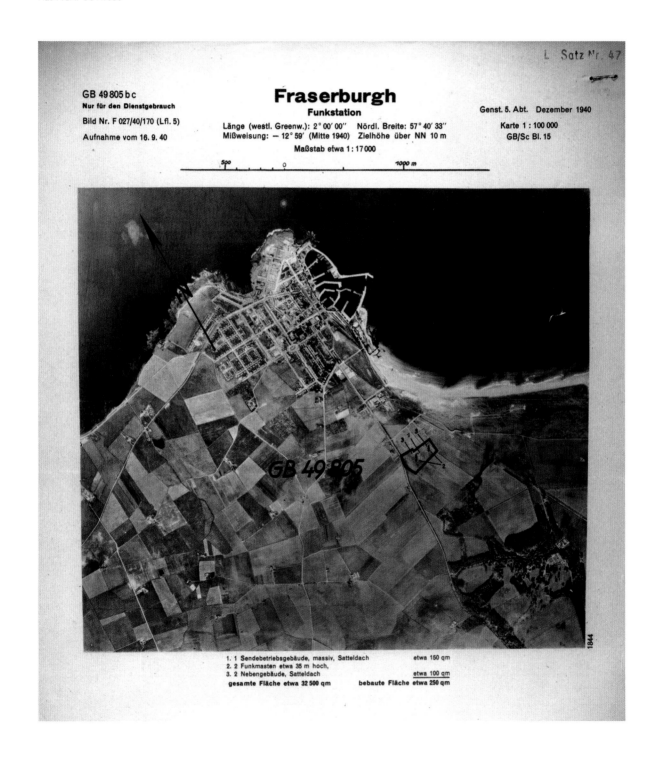

interest in this, however, most of his questions were about the nature of the seabed there: whether it consisted mainly of sand or rock. Archie told him it was the latter, surmising that he was a spy looking for a place where U-boats might find shelter when or if war arrived.

This may have been a presentiment of what was to come. Fair Isle North was attacked twice during March and April 1941. In addition to the damage caused by machine-gun fire to the dwelling houses, two bombs were dropped on 28 March. They landed a short distance away from the tower and the only damage that was done was broken glass. On 18 April, another attack took place. Again, two bombs were dropped, demolishing the outhouses and much of the boundary wall.

Yet nothing compared to all that happened to the Fair Isle South lighthouse the following winter. Catherine Sutherland, the 22-year-old wife of the assistant lightkeeper, was killed by machine-gun fire as she stood at the pantry window; her infant daughter slightly hurt. On 21 January 1942, the German planes were back again. On this occasion, Margaret and Greta Smith, the wife and ten-year-old daughter of Principal Lightkeeper Smith, were killed when there was a direct hit on the main dwelling block, completely burning it down. On his way back from the island post office at the time, the keeper was powerless to protect his wife and child, observing the destruction after he returned. He could only bear witness to both the loss of his family and the death of a soldier, William Morris, who was manning a nearby anti-aircraft gun at the time. Just as remarkable was the response of Roderick MacAulay, the assistant keeper of Fair Isle North, who made his way through gale force winds and snow to restore the Fair Isle South light. It was an endeavour which merited him the British Empire Medal.

The lightkeepers stationed there and in other locations throughout Shetland during 1940 also probably observed some of the 30 boats that took over two hundred refugees, including women and children, from Norway to Shetland, fleeing the Nazi regime that had occupied their country. They were silent onlookers, too, as they gazed on the men and boats of the Shetland Bus, members of the Norwegian resistance who set up base in Lunna on Shetland's north-eastern coast. They employed these vessels to sail back and forth to Norway for the first year after their arrival in Scotland, operating a clandestine shuttle service, delivering radio sets, agents, ammunition and arms to those who remained behind. While doing this, they sailed past various landmarks, such as the lighthouse in the Out Skerries, to the Norwegian coastline, sometimes returning with a boatload of refugees. Later, they moved to Scalloway where they continued their resistance to German rule. By November 1943, they made this voyage not in the few remaining fishing boats but in three fast sub-chasers, 100 feet (30m) long with a top speed of 22 knots. As they bristled with arms, German aircraft made every effort to stay away from them. As a result, all three sub-chasers survived the war.

Shetland, of course, was not the only place where lightkeepers were affected by war. Recording his time at Buchan Ness lighthouse near Peterhead, Archie MacEachern recalled the aftermath of an incident in which a German U-boat had been blown up by its own devices while laying mines in the shipping lanes off the coast. A fishing boat picked up the majority of the survivors. However, together with his fellow lightkeeper, Archie witnessed a raft with a single occupant sinking a short distance from the shoreline, unable to save the man aboard from storm and sea. He was then asked by the Home Guard to assist in the rescue of two others from the U-boat, helping to haul them by rope from the foot of a cliff. The first man was rescued easily. The other, however, collapsed and died a short time after he reached the summit. It was an encounter that had a profound effect on MacEachern, who concludes this account with the words: 'He was too young to die and I have never forgotten him.'

Most of the time, however, lightkeepers were fated simply to be observers. They did this in both conflicts and – sometimes – their aftermath. In Orkney, those at Hoxa Head or the lighthouse on Hoy must have raised their binoculars in bafflement as they stepped out on the gallery around midday on 21 June 1919. Some time after Germany's surrender, the German Imperial Fleet was beginning to sink in the shelter of Scapa Flow, their mainmasts listing as the vessels were transformed into grey rocks and skerries, their keels and hulls all that remained of them as steel seeped into the depths. Its commanders had ordered this to take place, rather than allowing their ships to be taken over and used by the Royal Navy. The keepers must, too, have watched with even greater horror at the devastation caused by the sinking of the

Royal Oak, where 835 men lost their lives in October 1939, noting the corpses washed up on the shoreline, contemplating the destruction, and wondering how on earth such horrors had taken place as they carried out their duties.

A similar experience was endured by some of the lightkeepers on the Isle of Lewis in the aftermath of the First World War when a bleak and desolate dawn on 1 January 1919 rose over some of the 200 dead from the *Iolaire*, all drowned on their voyage home from the conflict. In their case, the grief must have been intensified in the days and weeks following the tragedy by the suggestion that it might have been caused by the officers on the *Iolaire* becoming confused between a number of the lighthouses they passed on their voyage. This was one particular theory put forward by the Admiralty. Anxious to deflect any responsibility for the incident, they claimed that some lights – including Tiumpan Head, Milaid Point and the tiny Arnish lighthouse – 'might not have been in order'. As the inquiry established, there was no truth in this story for all that it must have made the lightkeepers question their own role in the deaths of these local men so close to home.

And then there are the west Highlands and Inner Hebrides, which over the years of war during the last century experienced a series of dramatic disasters. One was the sinking of the US Liberty ship the *William H Welch*, which hit a rock when returning to Loch Ewe on the morning of 26 February 1944. Two of the lightkeepers from Rubha Reidh joined the local crofters and their families to try and help the American crewmen who scrambled to shore on that day of cold and blizzards, bringing blankets and tea. Only 12 survived who were on the vessel: the remaining 62 perishing either in the depths of the waves or on shore.

There were also incidents like the sinking of the *Arandora Star* on 2 July 1940, 75 miles west of County Donegal, when 865 lives – mainly of German and Italian internees – were lost, their bodies scattered and sometimes found throughout a host of locations, such as the north of Ireland, the island of Colonsay and the coast of Kintyre. Archie MacEachern provides his own account of this, writing of his days in the tidal island Erraid, off the shores of Mull, where there was both a signal station and a row of nine keepers' cottages for the families of the men who were stationed on either Dubh Artach or Skerryvore. He notes that a great deal of wreckage from the *Arandora Star* was washed up on that island. It included thick mahogany doors and planks, wash basins with wooden surrounds, and 'a sturdy ship's boat' which arrived in Erraid 'empty apart from a child's shoe and a jacket'.

This must have been another of the occasions when even tough, resilient men like Archie MacEachern did not keep their gaze upon the waters but blinked and looked away …

IN SALUTEM OMNIUM

18 99

Chapter 7
Life Within the Gates of Death
Dramatic Tales from Scotland's Lighthouses

Those that go down to the sea in ships,
that do business in great waters,

These see the works of the Lord,
and his wonders in the deep.

Psalm 107

'Half a man. That's all I was in terms of wages.' Peter Johnson chuckles as he recalls how little he and his cousin earned when they worked on the lightship together 70 years ago, delivering supplies to the lighthouse on Bound Skerry in the Out Skerries where he grew up. 'Five shillings a trip. Out of which we paid fivepence as insurance for any industrial injuries we might suffer as a result of anything that might happen on board. We considered ourselves lucky to get it. The work only came our way because there was a shortage of men.'

Now in his mid-80s, Peter has spent much of his life at sea. In working terms, its hold and sway over his

Lightkeepers' Dwelling Houses, Breasclete, Lewis, Na h-Eileanan Siar B Listed

In villages like this one on the west side of Lewis, the Northern Lighthouse Board offered a gateway to a new way of life, giving those who enrolled in the organisation a wider horizon and more secure employment than the inhabitants had ever experienced before.

1896 drawing NLB Canmore DP038539

existence began when he and his cousin left school at the age of fourteen or fifteen. ('I'm not sure which,' he declares.) It continued through his later employment. This included the period when – after his National Service – he returned to the Skerries to work, building boats and houses there. Then there were 30 years on the fishing boat *Wavecrest* and the fish farm where he worked from 1986 till his retirement. He looks back on a life in which he must have spent many days on boats shivering in the winds that prevail over these islands, mornings when he rose and the sky was as great and murky as cold porridge, when the wind had the sharp swathe of a scythe.

It is fortunate that Peter has both the frame and will to stand steadfast in the kind of weather that often afflicts the north of Scotland. Even at his age, he has the confident stride and bearing of a man endowed with physical strength. His faith too is crucial to his existence. Every week, when his health permits, he attends the local Baptist church in Lerwick a short distance from his home, part of the rituals of a life that, through all its gusts and storms, has been anchored in the Bible and its teachings. Together with the sea, this has been a feature of his life since his schooldays in the Skerries. When he left his classroom desk behind to work on the lighthouse boat, he was following a family tradition. Many of his relations had lighthouse connections. On one of the first occasions he spoke to me, he mentioned an aunt who married a man called Angus MacCuish from Harris, once the lightkeeper in the Butt of Lewis. Another aunt, Annie Henderson, was married to a Hebridean called Norman Macleod, who came to work in the lighthouse at Skerries for a time. There were other relatives, however, who had stayed close to home. They included John Henderson – who was employed as assistant keeper – and Willie Anderson, who also worked as boatman there.

Reflecting on his own lighthouse activities, Peter recollected, 'We used to deliver coal and water to the lighthouse. Loading the coal onto a bogie when we arrived there. There was a pit for the coal at the underside of the tower. The water was stored in the lighthouse in the base. We hauled it up there too. Hard physical work.' It was a task that had been performed to fuel the light since it first shone from the islet of Bound Skerry in 1854. Curiously, like its other, better-known northern counterpart, Muckle Flugga, this lighthouse appeared as a result of the Crimean War, built at the request of the Royal Navy. (A temporary light shone on Muckle Flugga from 1854 – the permanent light atop its 64 feet (20m) high brick tower was built over the next few years, appearing for the first time on 1 January 1858.) There is no doubt that it was a necessary construction – though not just for the reasons the military authorities gave at that time. If the waters around the islands where Peter was raised were ever drained or emptied, a vast number of submerged ships and other horrors would come to light. They would include older vessels such as the Dutch East India Company's *Kennemerland* wrecked off the Stoura Stack in the Out Skerries back in 1644 with only four survivors – all on look-out as the ship went down – and a great deal of spoils for the locals and the islands' owners to quarrel over. It is an incident that is still part of the folklore of Shetland's islands, recorded in verse.

> The Carmelan frae Amsterdam
> Cam on a Maunmas Day[1]
> On Stoura Stack she broke her back,
> And in the Voe she ca'

A Danish ship called the *Wrangels Palais* sank a few decades later in waters close at hand. Of the 240 crew on board, at least 88 perished. It is due to the sinking of these vessels that this section of the seabed has been designated a Historic Marine Protection Area. This recognises this stretch of water as containing 'the best preserved and best recorded examples of the numerous wrecks of vessels of international origins that are known to have occurred in the waters around Shetland during the 16th–18th centuries'.

These vessels were not alone. Records suggest that throughout this period there was the loss of some 75 vessels of various north European, French and Spanish origins around Shetland. Among them was *El Gran Grifón*, the flagship supply vessel of the Spanish Armada, which was shipwrecked against the overhanging cliff of Stroms Hellier on Fair Isle in 1588. Another was the Dutch vessel *De Liefde* in 1711. We are told its cargo included 227,000 guilders in bags, over £4.2 million today, and 'Of these some 2,000 guilders were salved by the local inhabitants during the year the ship sank.' Of those on board, there was one survivor – the sailor who was on look-out at the masthead at the time. He was found wandering the island cliffs by the only person there who did not attend church that morning.

Even in comparatively modern times, the danger inherent in these waters has persisted. Peter tells me about how his uncles were involved in the rescue of men from the German ship the *Northwind* in 1906. Three men perished on that vessel; seventeen survived. The islanders benefited in certain ways from this encounter. Some of Peter's relatives and a few other residents received two sovereigns for their part in this rescue. They also obtained the vessel's cargo. Houses and other structures were reinforced with the cement on board, and the timber provided flooring.

Yet it is the legacy of events on 18 January 1912 that had a greater impact on Peter's forebears. It was, according to all accounts, part of a period of extreme weather which had continued for quite some time. The Lewis correspondent for the *North Star* complains about this, how the 'old year departed weeping' and how 'wretched weather conditions still prevail'. In the same Highland newspaper, there is a news report obviously cribbed from the insurance underwriters Lloyds which notes that 'almost every steamer reaching port has come with extensive damage to fittings and cargo'. It goes on to conclude that 'the recent terrific [sic] weather is responsible for the largest overdue list which Lloyds has had the misfortune to study for quite some time'.

---

1 The feast-day of St Magnus, now celebrated on 16 April.

Fair Isle (South) Lighthouse, Shetland B Listed

In 1998, the 200-year-old tradition of employing lightkeepers came to an end here at the southern end of Shetland, near the wreck site (foreground) of the sixteenth century ship *El Gran Grifón*.

HES Canmore DP260033

Although conditions were bad over Britain and Ireland as a whole, they were even more severe in the north-east – the icy summits of seas, their steep depths, the wrangle of tides, all ushered in by shrill south-easterly gales. The swiftness and savagery of these storms brought about many losses. Among a litany of boats and vessels which were overcome by the waves, there was the *Sublime* from Buckie, the *Frederick Snowdon* from Peterhead, the *Wistow Hall*, which sank in the vicinity of Port Erroll, and the barque the *Adele* off Scaw Rock in South Ronaldsay, Orkney. Over 70 lives were lost in these incidents alone over the five days from 15 to 19 January.

And in Shetland, if it were possible, conditions seem to have been even more difficult. At a time when the winds seem to have broken all their moorings, a host of ships were damaged or wrecked, including the *Swallow* and *Devanha* from Scotland, and the *Zeus*

and *Professor Johnson* from Norway. On 14 January, the *Rapid* went down off Vidlin, the men from that township releasing the crew from the chains of wave and surge. All survived despite this vessel, a Peterhead trawler, being a 'total wreck or loss' which still lies within the shallows of the voe at Vidlin today. On 18 January, a short distance away, off the Skerries, there was – to quote one of the dramatic headlines from the *Shetland News* – a 'Swedish Barquentine Dashed to Pieces'. In this 'shipping disaster' – the sinking of the *Advena* – there were, as the dark toll of sub-headings in the newspaper goes onto declare: 'Five Men Drowned: Two Men Saved'.

This rescue was largely the work of Peter's relatives, who manned a small boat and rowed out towards the sinking ship. It was, according to the *Shetland News* report, a task that required both strength and daring. Half-filled with water, 'it could only be rowed with the utmost difficulty. The four men at the oars, however, bent to their work with superhuman effort, and eventually, succeeded in reaching the spot where the tragedy of the sea had been enacted. They saw two men, one on the keel of the lifeboat and the other holding onto a small piece of wreckage.' The rest of

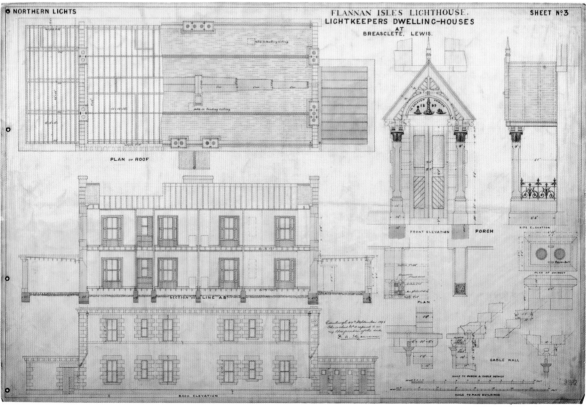

the crew had 'met their death' when the *Advena* went down. With great difficulty, the two survivors were brought on board and taken to the Skerries where they were cared for and looked after.

It was an action for which the men of the Skerries – including John Henderson and Willie Anderson – were well rewarded. The Secretary of the Northern Lighthouse Board, Edinburgh-born C Dick Peddie, captured their images when they received an award from the Carnegie Hero Fund during the annual lighthouse inspection voyages that year. Together with this, they also received £10 each for their part in the rescue, approximately £840 today.

They were not alone among lightkeepers in such acts of bravery. Another individual who displayed similar courage was lightkeeper Calum Macaulay, who worked in a variety of lighthouses across Scotland for many years, from St Abbs Head to Cape Wrath, Bass Rock to Sule Skerry. Like Peter, he was familiar with the trade from his early years. Brought up in Breasclete on the Isle of Lewis, his neighbours were those who occupied the Shore Lighthouse Station for the Flannan Isles lighthouse. Built in 1899, the two-storey buildings housing four families – 'two-up; two-down' – dominated the village, the crest with a flashing lighthouse and the inscription 'In Salutem Omnium' ('For the Safety of All') above its door. Looking back to his childhood, Calum remembered that, 'I went to school with a lot of the children who stayed there. Their way of life was familiar to me from an early age. Even the hours they worked. It was two months on, two months off at that time. Later it became one month on, one month off.' It was because of this familiarity that not only Calum but also his brothers Donald and Alex became lightkeepers. 'It must have got into the blood-stream,' he laughed. 'Or the atmosphere. There were a few men from the village who joined the Northern Lighthouse Board.'

In the course of his life-time's work, there were a few dramatic stories. Among them was a time in the

Lightkeepers' Dwelling Houses, Breasclete, Lewis

Urras an Taighe Mhòir – a community trust centred on the lightkeepers' dwellings in the village – took over the building in 2019 and plan to transform it in the coming years. Since being built as a shore base for the families of Flannan Isles lightkeepers in 1899, the listed sandstone building has been one of the area's most recognised landmarks.

HES Canmore DP004799, 1896 drawing NLB Canmore DP038539

early 1980s on Bass Rock when Calum heard his native Gaelic in the strangest of circumstances – a loud cry of '*Tha mo chasan fluich!*' ('My feet are wet!') echoing from near the island's landing stage. It turned out that the yell came from a boat bringing cement and other building materials to the rock. The load had shifted and the vessel began to sink. More affected by laughter than fear, the lightkeepers came together to help the crew ashore.

On the morning of 23 August 1965, during his first term of duty on the Pentland Skerries, Calum was involved in a more serious rescue. It took place during the early hours of a day when even the gulls sounded feeble and forlorn, the sharpness of their cries blunted by the weight of the mist that had fallen on the waters of the Pentland Firth. The light of dawn had apparently been cancelled or postponed. Only the blare of the foghorn the keepers had set in operation cut through the summer haar, warning the ships that sailed through that narrow channel of the weather conditions that prevailed.

Some heard it too late. Among them was Captain Horst Wentzel, the master of the 8,000 ton East German ship *Käthe Niederkirchner*. Aware of the note of the foghorn only when he was conscious he was both too close and on the wrong side of the Muckle Skerry, he tried to turn his vessel round. A few moments later he was alerted to yet another noise. It was his cargo boat grinding against stone below the keel, the pull of the tide too strong to avert the encounter. It didn't take much time for Captain Wentzel to be sure that his ship – with a hold full of sugar from Havana in Cuba – was destined to sink. He dashed off a quick SOS message before the radio failed and ordered the ship's lifeboat to be lowered. Together with Ajax the Alsatian, 48 individuals – 9 women, a six-year-old boy, 38 members of the crew – clambered aboard to sail to safety. (Other accounts refer to a total of fifty on board.) Some were dressed in their pyjamas and nightclothes. All had been forced to abandon their belongings on board the doomed ship.

It was at this point that David Leslie, the chief lightkeeper, and Calum became involved. Led by the Lewisman, the two shimmied down the cliff and into the lifeboat, piloting it to shore. With thick strands of mist still snarling the island's rocks, it was the only way they could ensure that the boat made its way to the landing stage, allowing all on board to step off onto dry land. No doubt the survivors all shook their heads and shivered, bewildered at the contrast between Muckle Skerry and their last port-of-call, Havana, feeling utterly disconcerted and lost.

Over the next few hours and days, life became more and more surreal for the lightkeepers as their lighthouse and the small island of Muckle Skerry became increasingly crowded. The first group of new arrivals were the men from the Longhope lightboat, who took the majority of the wreck's survivors back to Kirkwall, where they were clothed, fed and – shortly afterwards – put on a plane to London, the first stage of their journey home. There were two exceptions to this. The first was Bosun Edwin Westphalen, who was the owner of the dog, Ajax. He spent much of his time wandering round the island's shoreline with his Alsatian, waiting for the authorities to sort out the quarantine arrangements for the animal. The lightkeepers' other companion was Captain Horst Wentzel who, according to Calum, talked about the likelihood of being 'sent to the kitchen' as a result of his error in allowing the ship to sink. It didn't take the lightkeepers more than an hour or two to work out the exact meaning of the expression – the East German slang for 'prison'.

The next arrivals came in the *Hope* from South Ronaldsay. Those on board included the Receiver of Wreck (the official for wrecks and salvage in UK waters), a coastguard officer and a policeman. Assisted by fisherman Willie Mowat, they hitched up the *Käthe Niederkirchner*'s motorboat high and dry upon the rocks and brought it back to shore. The *Hope* returned between 9 and 10pm as twilight fell, the vessel intending to perform a similar action by towing ashore the two lifeboats that had become separated from the sunken ship. This was the prelude to yet another dramatic incident – one that gave rise to a thousand tabloid stories and the excruciating headline 'Pirates of Pentland'. Allegedly – in the words of lyrics from that musical – 'the foeman bared his steel', as a seine-netter fishing boat from Caithness sped in the direction of one of the lifeboats, seeking to haul it away from those who had salvaged it. A tussle – again allegedly – involving grappling hooks, axes and other forms of 'bared steel' ensued as those from the south attempted to claim the spoils, cutting the tow-rope in half. It was an incident that brought a further visitor to the lighthouse dwellings, joining the German captain, bosun and dog.

'Another policeman came to stay with us for a few days, just to oversee the wreckage and make sure it wasn't plundered.'

Yet, according to a later story, the entire happening could have been more dramatic still. Willie Mowat claimed that the sugar the boat was carrying from Havana to Rostock disguised a far more dangerous cargo. In a BBC interview that took place in 1998, he claimed that there was 'a strange metal cylinder with radioactive markings visible' on the vessel, 'fixed to the bottom of the hold'. He also said that his son, Lawrence, employed as a diver, had seen the container as he investigated the wreck in 1972, believing it to be one of the nuclear weapons sent to Cuba some ten years earlier at the height of the Missile Crisis. Hidden among sugar, they were being returned – supposedly – to the sites and bases from where they came.

Calum chuckled when I spoke to him about it, neither confirming nor denying the tale. All he told me was that nine hours after its first encounter with the Muckle Skerry, they heard a loud explosion as the boat went down, creating a noise more jarring and unexpected than the foghorn's notes.

'It was quite a blast …'

Even today, with all the benefits and advantages of modern technology, accidents still happen in the vicinity of the Pentland Skerries lighthouse. On 18 July 2018, for instance, we are told in an official report that the Netherlands-registered general cargo vessel *Priscilla* ran aground there.[2] For about two hours prior to the accident, the officer of the watch had been unaware that *Priscilla* was drifting away from the planned passage. The main reason for this? The accident apparently occurred 'because the officer of the watch was distracted from the critical task of monitoring the passage by watching videos on his mobile phone.' An additional factor in the accident was the fact that: 'He was the sole lookout at night as the vessel headed towards land, and the electronic navigation system was not set up to warn of danger ahead'.

Skerryvore lighthouse, too, played host to many of the passengers of the *Labrador* when that ship struck Mackenzie's Rock in early March 1899, providing both shelter and refuge for many of those whose voyage between St John's in Newfoundland and

2 See www.gov.uk/maib-reports/grounding-of-general-cargo-vessel-priscilla

Pentland Skerries Lighthouse, Orkney A Listed

The winds and tides of the Pentland Firth often delayed landings to this lighthouse. In 1871, a boy was rescued in the 'boiling tideways' off the Skerries, and it has since been the setting for a number of life-and-death dramas.

HES Canmore DP092218

Liverpool had been suddenly curtailed. A number of striking examples involved the Isle of May lighthouse, where a considerable list of men serving on that island became part of such ventures. The Royal National Lifeboat Institution, for example, rewarded the lightkeepers there for saving lives when the *Matagorda* was wrecked in 1872. The German government sent a set of binocular field glasses each to Robert Grierson and Laurence Anderson when they helped the crew of the *Pau*, which was lost on Inchkeith in 1888. In 1930 two young lightkeepers rescued four men by swimming in the direction of the Aberdeen trawler *George Aunger* wrecked on the North Ness and helping

them to come ashore. They were powerless, however, to help anyone in the so-called 'Battle' of May Island on the final day of January 1918, when a series of collisions involving a cruiser, the HMS *Inflexible*, and various Royal Navy K-class steam-powered submarines occurred in the waters nearby. Over a hundred men died because of the tragic and deadly farce that ensued. As a result of this and a number of other similar serious accidents, the submarines obtained the nickname 'K for Calamity' among the men of the Navy.

Sometimes lightkeepers themselves have been victims. An individual who suffered as a result of his time on Bell Rock was Principal Lightkeeper William Cordiner. Together with his assistant John Simpson, he was marooned there for a considerable stretch of time: eleven weeks in the case of Cordiner, seven for his junior officer. Their exile in February 1937 was caused by a number of factors, including the fury of the weather and a bout of influenza. For much of their time, they had the comfort of a new wireless telephone, introduced two years earlier. Although far better than signalling flags and flashing mirrors,[3] this had its limitations, with the batteries on which the system relied running out a few days before the end of their exile.

This was to prove a greater problem the following year. In November 1938, his fellow keepers radioed to inform the coastguards stationed at Fife Ness that Cordiner was ill with suspected appendicitis. This communication method clearly had two advantages over the use of semaphore. It allowed the lightkeepers to discuss with a doctor how to treat Cordiner's condition. It also permitted the Northern Lighthouse Board Commissioners' relief vessel, the *Pharos*, to be sent out immediately to take the principal lightkeeper to hospital. It was, however, an arduous and difficult process, especially as, strapped within a bosun's chair, Cordiner had to be lowered 9m from the door into the vessel. After this, he was transferred to the Arbroath lifeboat before being taken to the Royal Infirmary in Edinburgh. After enduring this ordeal, it is not highly surprising that he died a week later. His widow always maintained that this would not have been his fate if his fellow lightkeepers had used the wireless telephone earlier. When Cordiner had first shown symptoms of his illness, they had tried to conserve its battery by first employing the old-fashioned signal ball to alert the shore.

Other victims of the isolated nature of lightkeeping work included two men, James Milne and Ward Black, who were respectively the principal lightkeeper and second assistant lightkeeper of Monach Isles off the coast of North Uist. On 15 November 1936, they rowed their dinghy from the island of Shillay, where they served, towards the neighbouring tidal island of Ceann Ear – or 'East Head' – in order to collect the mail, a relatively short journey that involved a walk of slightly over two and a half miles. A cup of tea with the boatman delayed their return home. Their moment of relaxation provided just about enough time for the wind to stir and stiffen, rising from the force 4 it had been earlier. It changed its direction too, coming now from the north-west.

While Milne's 19-year-old daughter, Annie, kept the lantern alight, the First Assistant Alexander

Macmillan stood on the shoreline, watching the entire drama through the blur of wind and the white of a sudden snow shower. He set off rockets to alert others. He focused his telescope on the two men, seeing they were up to their waists in water about 150 yards from the shoreline with the boat lying on her side alongside them. In desperation, he waded into it with a navigational lamp in his hand, calling out for his two companions.

There was only silence in response – the two bodies of Milne and Black being found by the boatman Alexander Macdonald on 7 and 8 December, both washed up on the shoreline of Heisker.

Yet the darkest day in the history of the Northern Lighthouse Board began not during a time when the seas were as grey and unrelenting as flint. Instead, it emerged on 18 August 1960, a day when waves were calm and placid, when they slapped the shoreline of Little Ross Island off Kirkcudbright in a gentle, languid way. It was this pleasant weather, hours when sunshine and an occasional shower mixed and mingled, that prompted bank manager Thomas Collin to take his 19-year-old son David out on a short crossing on his dinghy to Little Ross Island. When they arrived, no one came to greet them on the shoreline. It was this absence that made the new arrivals uneasy, prompting the older man to make a courtesy call to the lightkeepers' dwellings to see if anyone was around. They received no response. Not even the persistent ring of a phone as they stood outside the lighthouse obtained an answer. No one appeared to be around. It was this that led to Thomas Collin's next action. He went into both dwellings, finding Principal Lightkeeper Hugh Clark lying in his bed. He was dressed in his pyjamas with a towel wrapped up beside his head, a few bloodstains splattered on it. After that, they rushed to the east quay where there were a pair of lobster fishermen on their boat. The group raced back again to the house where they confirmed there had been a death.

It never crossed their minds that there had been a killing …

That thought came later – when it was discovered that Hugh Clark had been shot at very close range by a .22 rifle. Afterwards it transpired that the weapon could only have been wielded by the hand of Assistant Keeper Robert Dickson. In response to what he had done, the young man fled the island on

---

3 The latter was heliographic communication and used for a few years at the beginning of the twentieth century.

Monach Lighthouse, Shillay, Na h-Eileanan Siar B Listed
Deserted since 1948 when the Morrison family finally left their
home there, a legend states that at one time these islands were
linked to North Uist by a sandbank, which was overwhelmed and
destroyed by a sudden and powerful storm.
HES Canmore DP258057

his superior's boat a short time afterwards, stealing
Clark's car and driving down to Yorkshire where he
was captured and arrested.[4] Later Dickson was put on
trial. Despite the fact he had a long history of mental
illness, he was – upon the judge's advice – sentenced
to death by hanging for capital murder. This was later

4 Jonathan Wills points out that, following this incident,
lightkeepers were banned from having their own boats in or
near their lighthouse stations. Regardless of this, during his
time employed on the attending boat at Muckle Flugga, he was
aware that one of their number, Sandy Wylie (mentioned earlier)
fashioned his own boat in the workshop on 'Da Rock'. Jonathan
suspects that this was shaped from the wood supplied to make a
coffin if anyone died while on duty.

commuted to a lifetime behind prison walls. It was
a penalty that was not inflicted on Dickson for very
long. He died by suicide a short time later.

Looking back 80 years later, it is apparent that the
tale of Little Ross Island has something in common
with the story of the loss of three men in the Flannan
Isles. Over the months and years following the date
the deed took place, speculation, gossip and horror
began to fill the vacuum at its heart. There were gory
and macabre rumours of how the deed had been
committed – that Clark had been shot several times,
his throat slit, his face blown away by a shotgun.

Perhaps this is a constant feature of a lightkeeper's
life, that certain fundamentals of his existence are
mysterious, that in a world in which so many of us
seek a sense of community, there is nothing more
strange and alien to us than an individual who
appears to turn his back on it.

In short, there is no better canvas for a story than
a horizon – whether it is blank or not.

Chapter 8
Fair Shines the Beacon
The Lighthouse in Art, Music and Literature

Fair shines the beacon from its lonely rock,
Stable alone amid the unstable waves

From Sir Lewis Morris, 'The Beacon'

Alongside either the *Oor Wullie* or *The Broons* annual that came one Christmas while I was in primary school, there arrived a special gift. Illustrated by the same individual, Dudley D Watkins, who was behind these characters in the *Sunday Post*, it was a copy of the children's classic *Oliver Twist* by Charles Dickens. The characters – Fagin, the Artful Dodger, Mr Bumble – etched themselves into my consciousness as I leafed through the book's pages again and again, reading the short pieces of prose that were typed below the pictures, trying to remember every word. 'Are there any more like this one?' I asked my Dad.

Six months or so later, three more, all sketched by the same illustrator, arrived in my home – *Robinson Crusoe* by Daniel Defoe, *Treasure Island* and *Kidnapped* by Robert Louis Stevenson. Again, I feasted on them, admiring the quality of the illustration, the power of their plots and characterisation. I even noted that

the storylines of these three books were connected. The central character of *Robinson Crusoe* was an Englishman marooned on a tropical island. There was a figure in *Treasure Island* called Ben Gunn who was in a similar plight, cursed with an insatiable appetite for cheese. And in *Kidnapped,* there was young David Balfour, trapped on a tidal island called Earraid near Mull after escaping from his imprisonment on the *Hispaniola*. It is a place which David believes is surrounded by salt water, impossible to escape from, only to discover a few days later after 'starving with cold and hunger for close upon one hundred hours' that 'a sea-bred boy would not have stayed a day on Earraid', for it could 'be entered and left twice in every twenty-four hours, either dry-shod, or at most by wading'.

There was a reason why this last particular scene had an effect on me, much greater, say, than Robinson Crusoe, his companion Man Friday or even Ben Gunn patrolling the island where he was exiled, feasting on coconuts and wandering around its palm trees. The scene in *Kidnapped* had echoes in my own locality. At the foot of one of the village crofts, Number 7 or 8, there was a tidal island called An t-Eilean Glas, its name adding a little linguistic confusion to the way it was seen, as the Gaelic words could mean either 'the grey island' or 'the green island'. It contained the two shades. There was a patch of green grass on its summit, with towers and turrets of grey gneiss around each side. As children we often scrambled up to its crest,

Isle Ornsay Lighthouse, Eilean Sionnach,
Highland B Listed

The cottages here – like their counterparts in Kyleakin – were once the property of *Ring of Bright Water* author Gavin Maxwell, who bought them in 1966.

Ian Cowe

stepping on and later sliding down the shingle the tide had washed up a short time before, slithering towards the rock-pools and boulders at its foot. We were always anxious not to spend too long on the summit, conscious of our parents' words and advice:

'So-and-so went up there one Sunday afternoon. It was the following morning before he got off there, his parents waiting for him on the shore.'

'Some fellows went out there fishing one evening. Didn't get back home till the following day.'

'Be careful when you go out to An t-Eilean Glas. It can be very tricky.'

And so each time I read that book, I identified with David Balfour, conscious that the mistake he made was one – in my stupidity – I could easily imitate. I could imagine what it must be like to be trapped on Earraid, unable to understand that where the sea rolls in, its waters must eventually sweep out again, leaving a (relatively) dry path behind. I could see, too, where the young Robert Louis Stevenson had obtained the imaginative basis for this idea. It was not only from visiting places like Earraid, where he spent time with his father and uncle while they were building Dubh Artach lighthouse, but also from listening to the tales of men who might have known similar situations, stranded for hours on end on a tidal island, waiting on its shore for the night to end and the passage of salt water that had trapped them there to ebb and disappear. There is, too, the notion that one of the sources for the novel *Treasure Island* was the young man's visit to the Muckle Flugga lighthouse, using the outline of the island of Unst to form the map contained within that book's pages. It seems to me that when or if Robert Louis Stevenson did this, he was drawing on a truth that lies at the heart of every lighthouse his relatives and others ever created. Every tower contains its own tales and legends, ones that were told by lightkeepers and sailors alike either at their places of work or within the inns and drinking places of ports not only in Scotland but throughout the world.

It is this idea that Jeanette Winterson deploys with great skill and lyricism within her novel

Erraid Shore Station and Observatory, Mull, Argyll & Bute C Listed (Observatory)

This island is known for its panoramic views, with Iona and the Ross of Mull to the north, and the Torran Rocks to the south. On a clear day, Dubh Artach lighthouse, 10 miles away, can be seen.

HES Canmore DP193392, DP193433

Lighthousekeeping. She introduces two of the characters from Stevenson's most famous novel, *Treasure Island*, in order to do this.[1] Pew becomes an employee at Cape Wrath lighthouse, maintaining the light there. Silver is a lost child, taken into this legendary figure's care. This confused and unsettled character is described as possessing:

> two Atlantics; one outside the lighthouse, and one inside me.
> The one inside me had no guiding light.

Yet Winterson does more than this in her dazzling, elliptical work – she also contemplates the entire notion of the lighthouse and its role in the lives of seamen and others. She points out, for instance, that whereas for officers the beams were a way of charting the vessel around the dangers of the coastline, they had a different function for ordinary sailors. The presence of these lights generated stories or even became one in itself – of vessels that sank near the rocks these towers guarded a long time ago, perhaps before the beams swept over the fury and fathoms of the sea, of everyday tragedies and miracles when lives were either lost or saved. These tales would be recounted and passed on 'from man to man, generation to generation', hooping 'the sea-decked world' before going back again.

And there is enough evidence that the existence of the lighthouse has inspired a multitude of stories. They include romances in which, say, the lightkeeper's daughter is a central figure, as remote and inaccessible as any princess sitting beside the battlements of a royal tower. There was, too, a plethora of films in the late 1930s and early 1940s which focused on these same structures around the coastline of the United States – a tradition that seems to have been revived again in recent years. This approach may have found its beginnings in *The Lighthouse*, a short and unfinished story by American author Edgar Allan Poe, who attended school for a short time in Irvine in Scotland. (This was spun out – beyond recognition – to be the genesis for a movie entitled *Edgar Allan*

1 She is not alone in using this book as inspiration. The former poet laureate Andrew Motion wrote two sequels to *Treasure Island* – *Silver: Return to Treasure Island* and *The New World*. The Swedish author Björn Larrson also wrote the swashbuckling saga *Long John Silver*. One could also argue that the *Pirates of the Caribbean* series of films are derived from this same source.

Poe's Lighthouse Keeper in 2016 with shambling zombie figures and a lightkeeper whose solemn injunction was to 'always keep a light burning'.) These lighthouse movies, almost invariably situated on a distant peninsula or island, are clearly similar to those that occur in Gothic towers and castles. One specific setting that might prove suitable for such an approach in a future feature is the lighthouse on the Isle of May, which manages to incorporate both concepts into its design.

One aspect of the lightkeeper's life that has generated a wonderful tale is the foghorn. The machine provides the title for a story by Ray Bradbury in which something entirely unexpected rises from the low cloud and sea fog, brought to the surface by:

> a voice that is like an empty bed beside you all night long, and like an empty house when you open the door, and like the trees in autumn with no leaves. A sound like the birds flying south, crying, and a sound like November wind and the sea on the hard, cold shore.

The above might be an excellent description of the way the foghorn sounds from Sumburgh Head. My friend J J Jamieson, a freelance sound recordist and filmmaker in Shetland, recorded its low growl with the aid of lighthouse engineer Brian Johnson. Initially he did this by pitching himself in front of it, trying to find the perfect place to capture its sound. Some time later, while working on the sound design for Robert Eggers' *The Lighthouse*, Damian Volpe saw this short segment of film. He contacted J J and asked him to record the sound once more. With the assistance of his children, J J recorded its noises again and again – from a quarter of mile away, a half-mile, a hundred metres – mingling it too with the mechanical noise the machine makes when it clicks into operation, the latch of a door closing, footsteps on the stairs, creating a soundscape for the film that is awash with terrifying and unsettling sounds.

Apart from Jeanette Winterson's approach, mentioned above, another considered way to write about lighthouses and their keepers is found in the novel *Pharos* by the Scottish author Alice Thompson. It takes place in Jacob's Rock, a small island on the west coast of Scotland. A ghost story, it seems to me to have links with the tales of the Blue Men of the Minch. These were rumoured to be men from Morocco and other parts of Africa taken home by Viking ships that once tied up in places like the Shiant Islands as they journeyed

Sumburgh Head Foghorn, Shetland A Listed
Built in 1905 and put into operation the following year, the foghorn was initially silenced in 1987, although it is now occasionally heard once again. Its orientation could be 'switched' to resound in the direction of where the fog had settled. This, however, was not always an advantage as it sometimes caused consternation and confusion for those sailing nearby.
REDA&CO / Contributor

through our waters. These mythical figures were said to haunt the seas, bringing vessels into the depths with them if the crew on board failed to complete a couplet of Gaelic verse. We are told in Donald Mackenzie's *Wonder Tales from Scottish Myth and Legend* how they could:

> skim along like salmon – you can see their shoulders gleam
> And the flashing of their fingers in the Blue Men's stream.

Alice Thompson also links the story with the slave trade, when boats from British cities used to take cargoes of shackled human beings from Africa

Isle of May Lighthouse, Fife B Listed

Nowadays the Isle of May is a National Nature Reserve. While upon its shores, visitors are asked to stay on tracks and paths to avoid disturbing the razorbills, eider ducks and shags that throng there every year.

HES Canmore SC1636472

across the Atlantic to the Caribbean and the United States to work in cotton and sugar plantations. She imagines a young woman called Lucia, one of their number, ending up on Jacob's Rock in the care of the lightkeeper. Without memory in the book's opening pages, she slowly begins to recall her past life as a slave.

Together with this, Thompson's novel glitters with insights about the nature of lighthouses and the work of the men employed to maintain the light. It notes, for instance, the central paradox of its existence, how 'as it shone across the sea in its generous circular sweep it meant both safety and danger at the same time', how it is as much a summons as a warning.

All this comes from a long tradition of Scottish writers, in particular, focusing their attention on lighthouses. This goes back to 1814 when Sir Walter

Scott travelled around the Scottish coastline for six weeks aboard the *Pharos* in the company of the Commissioners. He wrote a diary about the voyage, which was eventually published in a biography written by J G Lockhart, mentioning such figures as Bessie Millie, an old woman who lived in Stromness and made her living selling favourable winds to seamen. It was this voyage that provided the basis for Scott's later novel *The Pirate*, set near Sumburgh in Shetland's South Mainland.

And then there are children's books, where the lighthouse tower can play an important part. One of the most long-lasting of these is the *Lighthouse Keeper* series created by Ronda and David Armitage. More than 40 years after I first read to my children about the way Mr Grinling the lightkeeper obtained his lunch, these books are still popular and well-read, even if the technology and – indeed – the relationship between the married couple at the centre of the story have become a little outdated over the years.[2]

2 Jonathan Wills – mentioned in these pages – has also produced children's books based partly on his time in Muckle Flugga, with one entitled *Granny Linda and the Lighthouse*.

The lighthouse is found in Gaelic and Scots tales and folklore too. In Gaelic song, the lighthouse is often seen a symbol of nostalgia for a past life. We see this in 'Seòladh Dhachaigh' ('Sailing Home') by Donnchadh MacFhearghais – or Duncan Ferguson – who writes about both the Ornsay lighthouse and the Rinns of Islay in the song. Again in 'O Nach Àghmhor' ('Without Happiness'), the peaks of northern Lewis – '*Mùirneag ainmeil is beanntan Bharabhais*' (or 'Famous Muirneag and the Barvas Hills') – are likened to the way in which lighthouses are seen by vessels approaching the shore. There is, too, a version of the Gaelic song, 'Chì Mi 'n Tìr san Robh Mi nam Bhalach' ('I See the Land Where I was a Boy'), made famous by former Runrig singer Donnie Munro, that is reputed to be written by a lightkeeper. Known by his patronymic, Coinneach Dhòmhnaill 'ic Thormoid, he was stationed at Eilean Glas lighthouse in Scalpay between 1924 and 1928.[3]

Eilean Glas Lighthouse, Scalpay, Na h-Eileanan Siar A Listed

One of the four earliest to be built in Scotland, this lighthouse has stood on the east coast of Scalpay off Harris since 1789. It overlooks the narrowness of the shallow waters of the Minch at this point and is situated at the end of a long and scenic walk.
Ian Cowe

Apparently he composed this song during his hours of watch, looking out at his native Isle of Harris, including the village of Strond where he was raised. A Scalpay man, John – or Seonaidh – Morrison, also cast a nostalgic gaze at his own home island while working, among a number of other jobs, as a lightkeeper at the Isle of May and the Flannan Isles lighthouses. The song 'Eilean Scalpaigh na Hearradh' is just one of a number – in both Gaelic and English – he wrote during his lifetime. It remains popular today, having been recorded by bands such as the Whistlebinkies and Skipinnish in recent years. Another lightkeeper, Angus Y MacLellan, also wrote Gaelic verse while employed as a lightkeeper in Margaree Island off Cape Breton for 34 years. He drew on his experience of the sea while

3 This is undoubtedly where Norman MacCaig's 'Uncle Roderick' used to pass regularly with its 'mile of nets' and his 'cran of songs'.

creating lines like those in 'Fàilte na H-Aimsir do D D' ('Season's Greetings to D D'):

> *Is coltach sinn nar cuairt san fhàsach*
> *Ris an luing air bhàrr na stuadh.*
> *Uair gu h-iomainn anns a' ghabhadh,*
> *Uair mar eala bhàn na suain.*

> In our journey through the desert,
> We're like a ship on the deep.
> Now driven into danger,
> Now like a white swan floating.

The Scottish musician Alastair McDonald adopted a more irreverent approach, putting new words to a traditional song called 'The Mermaid's Tale', and setting the scene on Bell Rock. He makes the claim:

> My father was the keeper of the Bell Rock Light
> And he married a mermaid one dark night
> And from this union there came three
> A codling and a kipper and the other was me.

Kyleakin Lighthouse, Eilean Bàn, Skye, Highland B Listed

Erected in 1857, the lighthouse once lit up the narrow channel that took motorists 'over the sea to Skye'. It is now overshadowed by the concrete stanchions that hold the Skye Road Bridge.

HES Canmore SC493539

In folktale, the range of interpretation is more varied. It extends from the various ghosts, including squads of Vikings that were at one time said to haunt author Gavin Maxwell's Eilean Bàn lighthouse near Kyleakin in Skye, to intimations of death and loss. As I recall from my own childhood, these were often relayed to my fellow Gaels through the inexplicable appearance of lights, sometimes that of a bright candle. There is, for instance, the story of a man from Barra who foresaw a large halo of lights not far from his home. Believing this was a prophecy of the loss of his large family, he decided to go into exile from his native island. A short time later a lighthouse was built in the vicinity of his former home.

Yet it is in terms of a metaphor that the lighthouse really comes into its own. As such, it is employed again and again in works either written by Scots or set in Scotland. It stands, full of threat and foreboding, in *The Lighthouse* by Agnes Owens. It is deeply ambiguous in the rather vague version of Skye in Virginia Woolf's *To the Lighthouse*.[4] (Is that 'stark tower on a bare rock' a guardian of ships? A phallic symbol? A sign of man's controlling grip on the world?) It is, perhaps, fitting that some of the finest works about lighthouses and lightkeepers are written by those with the surname Stevenson. Robert Louis Stevenson wrote several poems on this theme, as befits a man from his family line of Scottish lighthouse engineers (his father being Thomas Stevenson and his grandfather Robert Stevenson) including these lines on 'The Lightkeeper':

> The brilliant kernel of the night,
> The flaming lightroom circles me:
> I sit within a blaze of light
>
> Held high above the dusky sea.
> Far off the surf doth break and roar
> Along bleak miles of moonlit shore.

One of the finest modern poems about lighthouses, however, was written by an Anglo-American poet, Anne Stevenson. Her work 'North East off Carnoustie' sums up the power of the lighthouse in a few concise words, including a reference to how:

> in far quarters of the horizon
> lighthouses are awake, sending messages –
> invitations to the landlocked,
> warnings to the experienced,
> but to anyone returning from the planet ocean,
> candles in the windows of a safe earth.

Yet it seems to me that the image of the lighthouse transcends the written word in a succession of ways. In visual art, it can – as in the work of the American painter Edward Hopper, who created several artworks featuring lighthouses near his home in Massachusetts and Maine – even be a self-portrait. According to the unflattering perspective of his wife, the painter Josephine Verstille Nivison, he chose to paint them

time and time again because they resembled his tall, stiff figure, distant personality, loneliness and impenetrable ego. The lighthouse can, however, also be a 'beacon of hope' as it was for professor of architecture Alan Dunlop who spent much of the lockdown of the years 2020 and 2021 sketching those around the Scottish coast.

In contrast, the lighthouse can also signify devotion, as can be seen from a story coming from South Rona, a small island lying at the northern end of Raasay in the Inner Sound off Skye. Apparently, a widow, Janet Mackenzie, used to keep a light in the window of her home in the mid-nineteenth century to prevent local fishing boats from having too close an encounter with rocks at the harbour entrance. (In some versions of the story, this was an attempt to make sure her husband returned home, as his vessel vanished and was never found.) Her vigilance was rewarded by the Northern Lighthouse Board who, after ten years of her lighting this lamp, provided her with £20 to help recompense the expense involved in her endeavour. A similar sum of money had been provided to her by Trinity House some ten years before. Since that time, the boat bringing supplies to the South Rona lighthouse has always been given her name.

The lighthouse can act, too, as a representation of selflessness, underlining the greatest and finest aspirations of mankind, as can be seen in the way the building is often portrayed standing on the horizon, its light aspiring to the heavens. This portrayal is underlined by the words of George Bernard Shaw, who among his less controversial declarations announced:

> I can think of no other edifice constructed by man as altruistic as a lighthouse. They were built only to serve.

And it is an icon of faith. It illustrates a way of guiding us through storms and the fog of doubt, summed up in the words of John 1, verse 5: 'And the light shineth in darkness; and the darkness comprehended it not.'

The lightkeeper performs[5] their own part in all this. They stand at the rail of the gallery, just before

---

4 Apparently its real inspiration lies in the light on Godrevy off the north coast of Cornwall which Woolf could see from the holiday cottage where she stayed as a child.

5 There are a number of reasons for writing about lightkeepers in the present tense. They still exist in literature and contemporary conversations as well as being employed in various locations throughout the world. According to Jazmina Barrera's book *On Lighthouses*, there are, for instance, 300 still employed on the coastline of her native Mexico.

the lamp, and watch all that is going on. They watch the way the tide twists and turns, noting whether the clouds are cumulus, stratocumulus, nimbostratus. They note the geology of cliff-faces, the lay of the land which stretches out behind them, its flora and fauna. They see the birds – gannets, fulmars, kittiwakes, as well as those like oystercatchers, turnstones and curlews found along the coast. They possesses a different viewpoint from the rest of us, more remote and distant, perhaps more objective …

The lightkeeper is an individual aloft and made different by isolation.

An observer of our world.

Island of Rona Lighthouse, Highland B Listed

Shrouded by mist, the coastline of Staffin in Skye forms part of the dramatic and impressive backdrop to this unusual lighthouse.

Ian Cowe

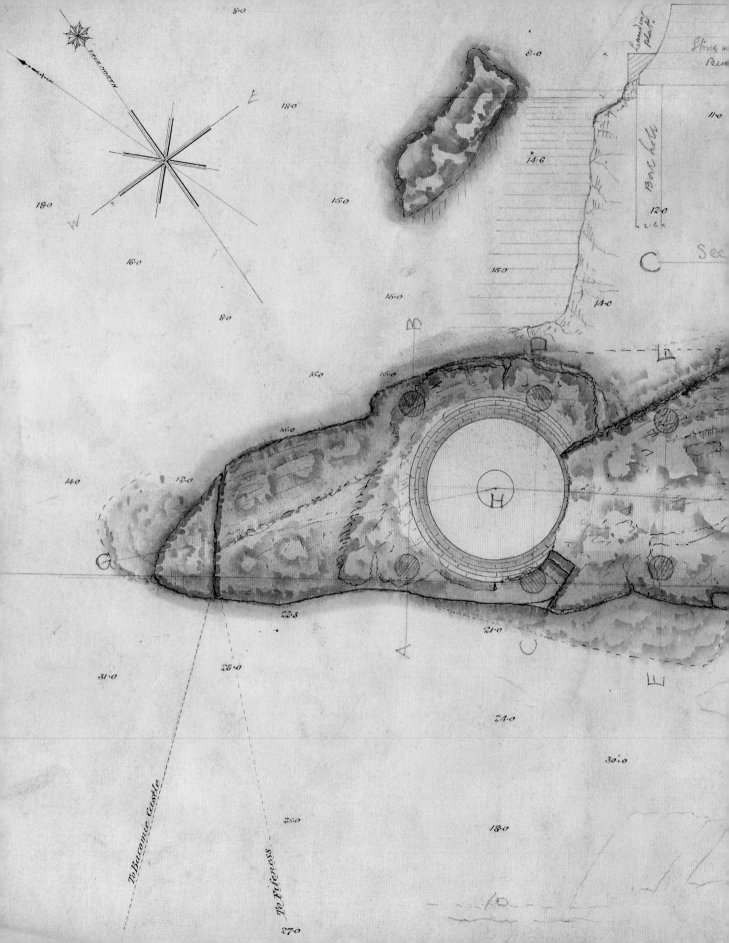

Chapter 9
Within Sight of the Sea
Innovation and Tradition in Scotland's Lighthouses

Like a pilot who sleeps best by a runway,
I sleep easiest within sight of the sea.

From Gavin Francis, *Island Dreams:*
Mapping an Obsession

'Dogger. Rockall. Malin. Irish Sea …' The words the Irish poet Seamus Heaney recalled in his poem 'The Shipping Forecast' were also part of my childhood. Together with my uncle, I used to listen to the BBC Home Service on our old wireless in the sitting room, focusing on words that reflected our geography in the Western Isles, Rockall, say, and Hebrides. We would hear predictions of the wild weather storming in our direction – prophesying winds at south-easterly 5 to 7, increasing to gale 8 at times later, sea state moderate or rough, rain at times in west. It was the verbal equivalent of the lighthouse at the Butt, issuing warnings to all who lived within sight or hearing of the waves, creating its own concise stories about the storms or the short periods of calm that were blowing our way.

Beacon, North Carr Rock, Firth of Forth, Fife B Listed
Made up of some fourteen sandstone rocks that are submerged at high tide, the reef stretches for 1.5 miles (2.4km) from Fife Ness into the North Sea and the greater Firth of Forth. A constant danger to ships over the centuries, the rocks have names such as Englishman's Skelly, Kneestone, Tullybothy Craigs, Lochaber Rock and Mary's Skelly.

1883 survey drawing, NLB Canmore DP280501

My experience of this time is one shared, too, by Philip Robertson, a marine heritage specialist, who is now employed as Deputy Head of Designations with Historic Environment Scotland. Listening to the Shipping Forecast on the radio was an important aspect of his childhood. His father, however, did not just focus – like my uncle and me – on the few names where the twists and turns of weather might affect our activities the following day. Instead, he listened to the weather conditions about to occur in a whole range of areas that would have sounded impossibly exotic to my ears, from Viking to Faeroes, Forth to Southeast Iceland. The reasons for this? Generations of Philip's family had been involved in shipping round our coastline and beyond from the mid-nineteenth century to the early 1970s, his great grandfather William Robertson being the original founder of the Gem Line of Glasgow in 1852. It was a company whose vessels bore a certain similarity to the Spanish galleon mentioned in John Masefield's poem 'Cargoes' with its hold containing a 'cargo of diamonds, emeralds, amethysts / topazes, and cinnamon and gold moidores'.

In contrast, the Gem Line ships bore names like *Ruby, Pearl, Topaz, Sapphire* and *Emerald* while carrying more mundane products such as coal, iron ore and limestone.

For all that the family's connections with the Gem Line ended in the early 1970s, Philip – throughout his working life – has continued his involvement with the sea. It was part of his existence during the ten years he worked at the Lochaline Dive Centre in the Sound of Mull. It remains part of his life today. Having originally trained as an archaeologist, Philip used the knowledge he gained from his studies to move into the emerging field of maritime archaeology, investigating the many wrecks – from the *Dartmouth*, sunk in 1690, to the late nineteenth century SS *Thesis* – found in Scotland's waters, assisting others to gain an awareness of not only the remains of underwater vessels but also the sea-life found within its depths and shallows. He developed these skills further when he began working for – what was – Historic Scotland in 2005. He was involved in advising the Scottish Government on the creation of Historic Marine Protected Areas and putting forward suggestions for this new designation, including important locations such as Drumbeg Bay in north-west Sutherland, which contains the wreckage of a Dutch vessel wrecked sometime between 1650 and 1750, and the HMS *Campania*, which now lies beneath the waves off the coast of Fife after being wrecked in a storm in 1918. Once a Blue Riband-winning transatlantic liner, the *Campania* was converted by the Admiralty for military use in 1915 – in May of that year the first flight from an aircraft carrier with a permanent flight deck took place from the ship.

Lighthouses are an important part of the legacy Philip seeks to protect. He talks about the structures with enthusiasm, speaking about their importance to our heritage. Philip explains that Historic Environment Scotland is responsible for 'listing' buildings which are of special architectural or historic interest. This means that these buildings become legally protected and changes to them are managed through the planning system. Contrary to popular belief, it doesn't mean that buildings can't change or adapt, but it does mean that careful thought will go into ensuring that any changes take into account the special character of the building. He does, however, go on to discuss much, much more than this. He explains that listed buildings tell us about who we are, including our cultural identity and sense of ourselves as a people. Lighthouses were not simply stone columns that documented how sailors and fishermen were assisted in steering around and traversing the frequently stormy waters around the Scottish coast, but 'Like many historic buildings, they also provide the story of how man navigated through time. They show a long tradition of how we innovate both to overcome difficulties and to take advantage of change.'

At present, Philip is engaged in working with the Northern Lighthouse Board, reviewing the listed building records of some of Scotland's most famous lighthouses as well as assessing unlisted lighthouses for designation. There are around 150 listed lighthouses and many more listed structures associated with the sea, such as harbours. He mentions how, for instance, it is important to remember that there were historic difficulties in the creation of certain lighthouses that stand around our coast. To illustrate this, he refers to North Carr between the Firth of Forth and St Andrews Bay, where Robert Stevenson first became involved in 1813 in building a tidally operated bell tower. It proved an even greater challenge than Bell Rock. Often covered by the sea even at low tide, work could only proceed irregularly, some two or three tides every fortnight. While it was under construction, parts of the stone structure were swept away on three separate occasions, during storms in 1815, 1816 and 1817. It was this that led to the design being altered, changed to a pyramidal structure of cast iron columns with a ball on top. By the time it was completed in 1821, £5,000 had been spent on its creation and Robert Stevenson regarded it as his first failure.[1] It is still visible today.

This development had its own legacy, the sea-beacon at North Carr becoming the forerunner of a number of others placed on various rocks and skerries around the coast of Scotland by David Alan Stevenson. These included the Halliman Skerries at Covesea near Lossiemouth, the Riv on the north coast of Sanday in Orkney, and East Vows near Elie on the Forth. Each possesses a cage on its top, known as a 'chair of refuge'. The East Vows cage was designed to accommodate eight to ten mariners if their vessel was wrecked nearby.

And then there are the lighthouses Philip lauds in his conversation as important ones for the nation to recognise and recall. He includes – like most people I encountered – the more 'romantic' and impressive creations like Bell Rock, Ardnamurchan, Skerryvore and the square-shaped Eshaness on the north end

1 In later years, the tower was augmented by the North Carr lightship, first put on station in 1889; its last successor is now found at the waterfront in Dundee. Fitted with a light and foghorn, it was built in 1933. On 8 December 1959, it was at the centre of a tragic incident in which the eight men of the Broughty Ferry lifeboat were drowned. The lightship was retired from active service in 1975.

Halliman Skerries Beacon, Moray B Listed

Following a storm in the Moray Firth in November 1826 when 16 vessels were sunk, a grid iron tower was initially erected on the Halliman Skerries in 1845. The following year, the Covesea Skerries lighthouse was completed.

NLB Canmore DP352564

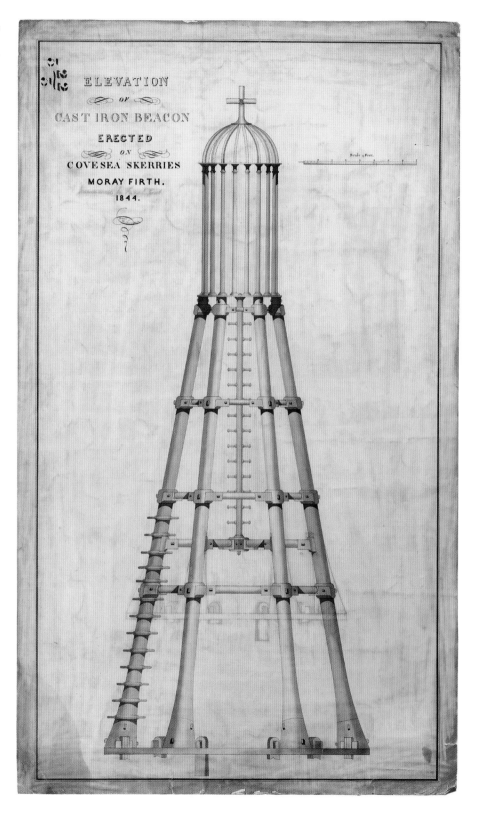

ELEVATION
OF
CAST IRON BEACON
ERECTED
ON
COVESEA SKERRIES
MORAY FIRTH.
1844.

Scale of Feet.

of the Shetland mainland, splendid in magnificent isolation. He also mentions Strathy Point at the northern edge of Sutherland, a prime example of how the Northern Lighthouse Board continued the long tradition of innovation they developed over the last few centuries. Built in 1958 and closed in 2012, it was the last manned lighthouse to be constructed in Scotland and is strikingly modern in appearance, complete with five layers of outside steps that lead to the heights of the tower. It was the first to be electrically operated from the outset, possessing a two-panel device with a focal length of 250mm and a 250 watt light bulb, giving it a range of almost 26 miles.

There is another at the opposite end of the spectrum which Philip also brings to my notice. It is the Sir William Black Memorial lighthouse, built on Duart Point at the most easterly point of Mull, to commemorate a now almost completely forgotten Scottish novelist of the late nineteenth century. First lit in 1901, it is a small castellated Gothic tower built of granite that stands on what was apparently Black's favourite place. Designed by Scottish architect William Leiper, it gleams only a short distance away from another light, the Lady's Rock light, one that could have been the setting of a Gothic story. Apparently that location obtained its title from the legend of Lady Catherine Campbell, the wife of one of the first Lords of Duart, Lachlan Maclean. She was stranded on the rock after displeasing her husband. In one version of the story, good fortune prevailed when her cries of distress were heard by a passing fisherman. She was not only rescued by him, but the fisherman also became her husband following her first husband's murder at the hands of her brother a short time afterwards.

Whatever the truth or otherwise of such stories, there is little doubt that there is much about lighthouses that would have seemed strange and surreal to our ancestors, especially those who lived in the Highlands and Islands. I was reminded of this when speaking to Tom Parnell, an architectural historian at Historic Environment Scotland. In our conversation, he spoke of the differences in the way we see these buildings from the sea and land. From

the ocean, these structures seem timeless, perched on shores and headlands overlooking cliffs and waves. This is not true of the manner in which we often view them from land – the long twisting roads through peat and heather that take us to Rubha Reidh at Loch Ewe, Ardnamurchan or the Butt of Lewis. There is something incongruous about them, as if plucked from the future – or sometimes, in the case of Duart Point and others, from a fabled and phantom past – and set down on these isolated edges of our coast. This was even more true in the age when most were constructed and placed upon the landscape on which they stand. The traveller making their way through my home district would have seen people going between byre and blackhouse, sheltering below thatched roof and behind low enclosures of rough stone. The lighthouse at the journey's end would have provided an entirely different perspective – one of concrete and brick, high and curved walls freshly painted, perhaps a crenellated tower or two. Even the brightness of the light that gleamed from its tower was of an entirely different quality from the Tilley and paraffin lamp found within most local homes.

The surreal nature of many lighthouses was also one of the impressions left with me after a conversation with Professor John R Hume, an expert in industrial archaeology who worked for many years as the Chief Inspector of Historic Buildings for Historic Environment Scotland's predecessor body. During his time in this role, he and his colleagues were responsible for surveying and listing many buildings, including lighthouses, railway stations and industrial structures, charting the changes that occurred to them over the centuries. A gifted artist and photographer, he recently produced a book entitled *Scotland's Lighthouses in Photographs*. In its pages, we see the sheer variety of lighthouses that have existed and still stand around our coastline. There is the unique structure of the now closed Holborn Head lighthouse, which I first saw as a teenager in Scrabster while on holiday with relatives in Caithness, its octagonal tower emerging from a square base that looked to me suspiciously like a domestic house. There are the front and rear lights of Torry Range, Aberdeen, the front one seeming small and slender standing beside the bulk of an oil tank, trapped, too, behind a high fence. And then there is the motley collection of harbour lights found in various locations like Gourdon, Findochty and Portknockie in the north-east of Scotland, the square walls of Duncansby Head in Caithness and my own favourite oddity, another unusual square lighthouse, Carraig Fhada in Port Ellen in Islay. Commissioned in memory of the late Lady Ellenor Campbell in 1832, it has a delightfully obscure verse on a plaque above its doors which reads:

YE: WHO 'MID STORMS AND TEMPESTS STRAY
IN DANGER'S MIDNIGHT HOUR:
BEHOLD WHERE SHINES THIS FRIENDLY RAY
AND HAIL ITS GUARDIAN TOWER:

John took these photos throughout his life, his passion for lighthouses beginning in his early teens when he was taken to the lighthouses on Little Cumbrae in the Firth of Clyde and Ardnamurchan on the westernmost point of mainland Scotland. Climbing the latter, he 'beheld the Hebrides' for the first time. His love affair with buildings deepened after that, leading to an interest in industrial archaeology – the ironworks, factories, canals and shipyards – which has followed him throughout his life.

Throughout our conversation, he stuck me as that rarity: someone who combines a diverse range of ability and skills. A man of science, whose initial academic studies involved applied chemistry, he was also inspired by a love of art. In this, in his own outstanding way, he resembles the majority of lighthouses that are found around Scotland's coasts, those like Girdle Ness in Aberdeen and Ruvaal in the Sound of Islay. They too combine an aesthetic sense with a deep understanding of the science and technology that was available to their creators at that time. It is not for nothing, as Tom Parnell pointed out to me, that Scotland's Centre for Design and Architecture in Glasgow is called the Lighthouse. 'The entire structure is an exemplification of that. Both design and architecture are intimately connected in all the lighthouses around our coast.'

Yet they are more even than that, as Tom's colleague Simon Montgomery told me. He visited a number of listed Scottish lighthouses during the last years in which they were manned, revising and updating their listed building records.

'Lightkeepers were the ideal custodians of historic buildings because of the amount of cleaning and painting they did,' Simon joked. 'I remember standing inside the lantern at Davaar lighthouse near Campbeltown in the Mull of Kintyre, looking out at the immense boundary wall freshly painted with white gleaming on both sides. It showed the attention to detail necessary in public service but it was also a splendid example of the Northern Lighthouse Board's pride in their buildings and work.'

Simon also visited the Mull of Kintyre lighthouse shortly before it was automated in 1996. Only two years before, a Chinook helicopter had crashed a short distance away from its walls, leaving 25 passengers and 4 crew dead. The earth on which it had fallen was still scorched and burnt, offering its own testimony of what had occurred. The principal

Davaar Lightouse, Kintyre, Argyll & Bute B Listed
At the mouth of Campbeltown, Davaar is an island only at high tide. At low tide, it is linked to the mainland by the Dhorlin, a bank of shingle. The lighthouse there was built in 1854.
HES Canmore DP069527, DP069550

lightkeeper, Hector Lamont, was among the first at the site, trying to find the victims of the terrible event. He was honoured with an MBE for his actions.

For Simon, his first view of the Mull of Kintyre lighthouse stands out in his memory because of the drama of its location, perched high above the sea on a narrow shelf in a bleak and rugged landscape. He recalled a conversation that had taken place with a keeper among the packed furniture and belongings stacked within the tower and lighthouse dwellings, some words that brought that earlier incident to mind.

'We've always been the eyes of the nation,' the lightkeeper had said, 'the first to see and react when things – bad and good – happen at its edge.'

Simon also recollected his visit to the Fair Isle South lighthouse on a crisp November day. 'I remember the exact date because it marked the return of the two-minute silence in 1996.' This was around a year and a half before Her Royal Highness Princess Anne was to address a group there to mark the automation of the only remaining lighthouse in Scotland that had not yet been subject to the process. The principal lightkeeper on that occasion was Angus Hutchison, an eloquent,

Angus Hutchison, Fair Isle (South) Lighthouse
Reflecting on the four generations that he and his family have been employed as lightkeepers, the late Angus Hutchison looks out on the Fair Isle coast.
PA Images / Alamy Stock Photo

able man who had been born in Sule Skerry lighthouse cottages in Orkney and was the fourth generation of his family to serve the Northern Lighthouse Board, having worked in locations ranging from the Isle of Man to Stroma and Fair Isle in the far north.

In a BBC interview recorded some time later, Angus summed up his feelings at the loss of both his job and the way of life it represented. Half-joking, he declared philosophically: 'When the Americans and Russians put satellites up in space, it was the beginning of the end. It was inevitable that technology would do away with ourselves.' He shrugged and smiled. 'After all, they don't need to look out the window now to see the Fair Isle light.'

On Simon's visit, with the keepers still at their posts, he recalled 'I was given a very warm welcome by Angus Hutchison and Bill Gault, who asked me

Northern Lighthouse Board Clock
Grandfather clock from the Isle of May lighthouse.
Allardyce Collection, Museum of Scottish Lighthouses

to join them for a cup of tea around their table to observe the silence. The room contained a magnificent Northern Lighthouse Board drumhead longcase clock. When I questioned Bill about it, he said "You mean the Auld Fella?"'

'It was a privilege to sit with the keepers observing the silence,' Simon continued, 'its passing marked by the tick of the old clock in the corner. A couple of years later, I was given a copy of the book *Scotland's Edge Revisited* by Keith Allardyce, which contains a photograph of the lighthouse clocks assembled in the Edinburgh depot for auction. They included the one Bill had called the Auld Fella. That, for me, was the most powerful representation of the loss associated with the automation of our lighthouses. A reminder, perhaps, that an old story had come to an end, a new one just beginning …'

Chapter 10
A Different Glow
Guardians of the Natural World

Oh! a bare, brown rock
Stood up in the sea,
The waves at its feet
Dancing merrily.

Louisa May Alcott, 'The Rock and the Bubble'

It was – in a roundabout way – a shipping disaster that brought Helen Moncrieff to work in Sumburgh lighthouse.

More than any other event, her choice of career was influenced by the sinking of the *Braer* oil tanker near Garth's Ness, a headland off Quendale Bay in Shetland, not far from either her home or, indeed, the lighthouse where she now works. It was an event that most of us who lived in the north of Scotland recall well – the whirl of winds that occurred between 8 and 17 January 1993, one of the worst that I can ever remember. There was the bite of a blizzard each time we stepped outdoors, the rattle of windows and the whoosh of the storm gusting off the chimney tops when we remained, cowering, in our homes.

Bass Rock Lighthouse, East Lothian C Listed

'It was an unco place by night, unco by day; and there were unco sounds; of the calling of the solans [gannets], and the plash of the sea, and the rock echoes that hung continually in our ears.' Robert Louis Stevenson's description of Bass Rock in his novel *Catriona* still holds true today.

Ian Cowe

And, of course, either on the TV screen or – for those who lived in the South Mainland of Shetland – the awesome reality of an oil tanker, which had lost its engine power some ten miles south of Sumburgh Head. Pushed and hoisted by the heft of waves closer and closer to land, its cargo of oil spilling, the strength of the elements such that the situation was well beyond the control of man. A dark sheen began to appear in the water, stretching north and south, staining sand and skerry. The black and venomous pellets of the 85,000 tons of light crude oil that were once contained in the tanker flooded the coastline, destroying the life that nested nearby or swam in the depths and shallows that were there.

A sixth-year pupil at the time, Helen's response to all this was to skive off school. Despite the chill of the wind and weather, and the stern disapproval of many of her teachers, she joined those engaged in gathering oiled wildlife and monitoring the dark spillage left behind by the vessel's sinking. There were various groups involved in this endeavour. They ranged from national bodies such as the Scottish Society for Prevention of Cruelty to Animals to the Royal Society for the Protection of Birds to local groups like Hillswick Wildlife Sanctuary and the Shetland Oil Terminal Environmental Advisory Group. There were those who arrived from outside Shetland, members of bodies like the Scottish Wildlife Trust and employees of what was then British Gas. Most of all, there were the ordinary people of Shetland, intent on saving their coastline from the damage that the sinking had wrought. Based in a Scout Hut near the tiny village of Boddam, they were organised into groups that walked local beaches to collect oiled birds and animals. When the wildlife was dead, they simply recorded and stored them. However, those that were alive were cleaned and dealt with – scouring the grey seal and the otter, the eider and the shag, ensuring that there was neither tincture nor tint of the oil they might ingest when preening their feathers. Among those who performed this task was young Helen, the experience confirming her attitude to her future.

'I always knew I would end up working in a caring role and the *Braer* experience helped confirm which direction to take,' she informed me. 'I didn't really want the blood and guts that might be involved in nursing and office life wasn't for me. Instead, I wanted to spend my time looking after the natural world, spending time outdoors and seeing the kind of birds and sea-creatures that were all around me in these shores.'

After completing her studies in conservation, Helen returned to Shetland and took up watch in the cluster of buildings alongside Sumburgh lighthouse with other members of the RSPB team. Much though she appreciates the sight of whales and porpoises occasionally breaking through the surface of the waves around the coastline of Shetland, it is the moments when familiar birds wing into her eyeline that give the greatest pleasure. 'Puffins. Guillemots. Kittiwakes. Twites … The kind of birds that come here regularly and punctuate the seasons. Moments, too, like the one I saw a while back. When a hen harrier was surrounded by maalies,' she said, using the Shetland word for 'fulmar'. She paused before speaking again. 'And, of course, there's the expression of joy that comes on some people's faces – especially the young – when they see these creatures. That's wonderful.'

Over the last few years, more and more people have been arriving at Sumburgh Head. Now owned by Shetland Amenity Trust, who took over its running in 2003, it was re-opened in June 2014 by Princess Anne in her capacity as Patron of the Northern Lighthouse Board. All spruced up, even the foghorn was given a new coat of paint, gleaming as if it were in use again. There is the Engine Room, the Smiddy and the Stevenson Centre – its wide panoramic views of nearby Fitful Head said to have inspired Sir Walter Scott to write the novel *The Pirate* when he visited Shetland

Wreckage of the *Braer* Oil Tanker, Shetland
The folk-rock group Fairport Convention commemorated the sinking of the *Braer* in their song 'The Islands' by declaring: 'We never feared the long ships, Till the coming of the Braer …'
PA Images / Alamy Stock Photo

in 1814. Like its near neighbours, Jarlshof and Old Scatness, it has drawn visitors from afar to this area of the South Mainland.

Yet Helen's joy at seeing the birds gathering and nesting there is increasingly tinged by her sense that she's not seeing as many anymore. She is aware that there has been a sharp decline in the numbers of kittiwakes, puffins, guillemots and other birds to be found in Sumburgh Head over the last few years. She is conscious, too, that there has been an alteration in the shade of the cliffs on which the tower stands, that it is no longer as white with guano as it was even a decade or so ago. There may be a debate about the reasons for this, from climatic change to overfishing, the effects, too, of plastic and other forms of waste in the ocean's depths. There is little hesitation in her voice when she comes to her conclusion. 'There's no doubt

Sumburgh Head, Scatness and Garth's Ness, Shetland
From this vantage point, it is possible to glimpse the past,
including the broch and Iron Age village that was uncovered in
the mid-seventies.
HES Canmore DP310579

that man bears a lot of the blame for this. We need to
live a bit more responsibly on this planet.'

In this sense, it is apparent that one aspect of
Sumburgh Head has not changed – its capacity to give
warnings. Its light may no longer caution fishermen
about rocks and skerries or its foghorn inform those
in vessels of the proximity of land. Nowadays,
however, the decrease in the number of nesting birds
in headlands like these advise us of changes that are
taking place both on land and in the oceans that brush
our shoreline. There are also events like one in the
latter days of 2019 when an adult sperm whale washed
ashore on Seilebost beach on the west coast of Harris.
An autopsy was performed on it which revealed a large
fishing net and rope within the mammal's stomach,
together with a great deal of plastic detritus – some
100 kilograms or 16 stone – including recyclable cups.

There is little doubt that this partly led to the whale's
final moments in West Loch Tarbert where onlookers
observed the manner it thrashed and flayed in the
waters there.

None can doubt either the importance of the
message we are being sent…

Those who work and live in lighthouses have not
always been such faithful guardians of the natural
world.

There is a wonderfully vigorous passage in the book
Hebridean Sharker which illustrates this, one in which
the writer Tex Geddes gives an account of a hunt for
basking sharks. The work, published in 1960, tells of
how, by employing an adapted whaling harpoon, he
and fellow crew members sought these creatures, some
over 9m long, in the waters of the Minch between the
Outer and Inner Hebrides, to obtain the oil contained
within their livers. It provides a revealing glimpse into
attitudes that are now almost all gone, doing so with
a verve and energy that belongs more to a sporting
occasion than the studied, calm observation of a
nature writer as he recalls a hunt that took place not
far from the north-west coast of Skye. It also reveals

the complicity of the lightkeepers of the time in this kind of adventure.

Away we went with a fair turn of speed clear out of the bay, when even the strong tide-race which flows around Neist Point did nothing to retard our progress, though it certainly would have, had we been under our own power. As we passed below the lighthouse, I looked up to see the three keepers out on the 'pulpit', obviously cheering us on, one of them waving a telescope round and round his head, but Johnny [McInerney, his companion] and I were unable to return his salute for we were both sitting on the foredeck with our feet braced against something, holding onto the harpoon rope behind the round turns on the samson post for fear of losing the lot. We certainly were a diversion and the keepers were later to tell me that they had prayed for a cine-camera, for from their high vantage point they apparently could not only see the shark just beneath the surface but the rope leading from it straight to the stem of the *Traveller*, and boring the tide which was dead against us, we appeared to be going much faster than we actually were.

Later in the book he visits Hyskeir lighthouse – called Oisgheir[1] in *Hebridean Sharker* – off Canna. The welcome they receive there at the southern end of the Minch is even more enthusiastic than the one they obtained in Skye. Perhaps, Tex Geddes suggests, their arrival is a 'break in the monotonous routine' for the three lightkeepers who live and work on the small island, as well as being useful for sending off their mail. Established in 1904, it was always a difficult lighthouse to reach by boat. A later example of this was seen during the winter of 1980 when bad weather stopped the lighthouse vessel *Fingal* from delivering ten barrels of oil on a variety of occasions between September and January. When these supplies finally landed, only two days' oil supply remained at the station. Whatever the reasons, the lightkeepers were more than helpful to Tex and his crew. He notes that:

1 Not to be confused with the island of Heisker (Eilean Heisgeir / Heisgeir in Gaelic), part of the Monach Isles, where a lighthouse also stands. The term Hyskeir is derived from *Òigh-sgeir*, the Gaelic for 'maiden' or 'virgin rock', and *sgeir* meaning 'skerry'.

Neist Point Lighthouse, Skye, Highland B Listed
Surely one of the most spectacular settings of any lighthouse in Scotland, Neist Point can be found by following a steep path on Skye's most westerly tip, near the village of Glendale.
Ian Cowe

Hyskeir Lighthouse, Highland
Constructed in 1904, five miles south-west of Canna, this was one of Scotland's more inaccessible lighthouses.
HES Canmore DP109421

They helped us remove eighteen hundredweights of liver from the shark. One of them cut a huge piece of skin, almost the entire belly which was mottled white and blue, with which he hoped to cover the back of a chair, and pictures of them standing on the back of the shark were taken for their families to see.

It was following this that – 'with the oil in barrels in the hold, and their letters to be posted', Tex and the fellow members of the crew sailed away on high tide, leaving the lightkeepers and the island behind them, no doubt cheered by both the company they had kept and the catch that had been brought with them.

It can be supposed that attitudes like these would have been common with lightkeepers at that time. Their views on nature would likely have been both inconsistent and utilitarian. This was not exceptional during the period. The well-known author and naturalist Gavin Maxwell was also a shark-hunter, and boasts in his book *Raven, Seek Thy Brother*, part of his *Ring of Bright Water* trilogy, that his boat, the *Gannet*, 'was the most successful harpoon-gun boat of all, and killed nearly two hundred sharks of almost her own length'.[2] Nowadays this statement would seem at odds with his love of wildlife, especially his fondness for otters, and the painstaking way in which he describes the wonders of the natural world. Not so at that time, where there is little doubt that lightkeepers would also have savoured the taste of cormorants, guillemots, gannets and the odd stray lapwing or snipe, together with the vegetables they harvested from the 'wonderful garden' Tex Geddes described existing on places like

2 The wonderfully eccentric Geddes also appears in one of Maxwell's less well-known books, *Harpoon at a Venture*. He was employed as Maxwell's first lieutenant and chief harpoonist in the Isle of Soay Shark Fisheries Ltd from the end of the Second World War until the company folded in July 1948.

Observing Bird Migration

'Here's a knocking indeed!' As birds thronged north or south, the peace of the lightkeeper's life was often disturbed by cries and the beat of wings.

1882 illustration – Universal History Archive / UIG / Bridgeman Images

Hyskeir. Plucked and boiled, these birds would have taken their place alongside the milk they obtained from goats or the eggs laid by the numerous hens that fed on grain lightkeepers brought with them, forming part of the diet that sustained them on the rock.[3]

This would have been particularly true on the occasions when supply boats like the *Fingal* failed to deliver resources to the men and the lighthouse where they worked. It would especially have caused difficulties in the era before the fridge or freezer became an everyday presence in kitchens both within the lighthouse dwellings and elsewhere. The lightkeepers would be compelled to fall back then on their own resources, attempting to bring a little variety to their increasingly meagre meals. They would look out at the landscape and seascape that were their surroundings, evaluating its worth not only in terms of its beauty, but also how it might provide for them in other ways.

3 It should be noted that in the case of the majority of these birds, numbers were greater than they are today. An exception to this rule is the gannet which now exists in larger numbers. The bird has even settled on locations like Sule Skerry in recent years.

There might be rabbits racing around the sand-dunes, but in some of the more isolated spots, such fare would be either rare or non-existent. There might be the brown tangle of seaweed, limpets and winkles or fish caught from the island rocks, but most of all, there would be seabirds – the cormorant or shag with the dark lustre of its feathers slipping into the waves, the gannet plunging from the heights, the guillemot among a myriad of its fellows on the edge of salt water.

As many of the lightkeepers were men from either the Scottish islands or coastline, the taste of these seabirds would have been familiar to them, a way of providing fresh – if salt-tinged – meat for the table when rations were spare or disappearing, a pleasant change from either canned food or heavily salted mutton which was probably their basic meal. It should be noted that they were unlikely to use the rather extreme menus one can find today. There is no record either of the lightkeepers training – as happened in China and elsewhere – any cormorants that landed on a nearby crag to catch fish. But that they ate them on occasion, especially in the nineteenth century, is undoubtedly true.

There were other occasions when, rather than the lightkeepers, the lighthouse towers were disruptive to the flight of birds. The book *Stargazing* by Peter Hill, possibly the most striking and individual account of being a lightkeeper in literature, tells of how he was awoken one night as he slept in Hyskeir lighthouse by a 'tapping and scratching at the window'. As a result, he arrived for his watch some twenty minutes early, witness to the most extraordinary of happenings, one that occurs twice a year – once, as noted here, when 'the land birds from Scandinavia [are] heading south to Africa for the winter'; the other time when they return in the spring. Peter describes this biannual incident in the most tender and mystical language:

> There were thousands and thousands of birds, circling in the beam of the turning light. Even from the ground I could tell they were of different sizes, different types, specks of wren and blobs of thrush and redwing. But they glided around so gracefully, as if on a carousel, the full moon appearing like speckled stars between their overlapping wings. I've never seen anything quite like it before or since.

Clearly haunted by the spectacle, one that must have resembled a version of Hitchcock's film *The Birds*, Hill goes on to describe the aftermath of that moment. The following morning, he notes that:

> most of the birds had gone, but one in a thousand had flown straight into the light like a moth to fire and broken their necks on the lighthouse glass.

It is his task to remove 'the dead ones from around the light', catching and freeing those that were still alive and terrified within the chamber. He lifted them, too, from the flat roofs of the lighthouse dwellings, providing them with a swift and unceremonial funeral at sea.

In the book, Peter Hill's friend and fellow-keeper, Mungo, puts forward the theory that this kind of event only happens to land birds, claiming that birds of that kind 'navigate their way south from lighthouse to lighthouse'. He wonders how they did this before these towers began to appear on peninsulas and islands, postulating the idea that they once migrated using only the stars and the earth's magnetic fields and are confused, bothered and bewildered by the existence of the lighthouse. Perhaps this is true. Despite his assertation, there exists a certain amount of evidence that some seabirds, particularly those that nest in burrows:

> are attracted to, and disorientated by, artificial lights. Light-induced landings can be fatal because collisions with human-made structures (eg buildings, electric wires, and pylons, fences, or posts) on the ground can fatally injure the birds.[4]

This kind of behaviour especially applies to seabirds like petrels and shearwaters. Their remarkable flights around the world can sometimes be either paused or ended in unusual circumstances. My friend Davie Ferguson has told me that shearwaters sometimes crowd the light chamber in Ardnamurchan lighthouse in a similar way to the ones described by Peter Hill in his book. In most instances, however, these collisions are not fatal. With a little help, the birds are only stunned and fly away a short time later, veering after darkness has faded once again in the direction of the Minch.[5]

4 Rodríguez *et al* 2017
5 Many lightkeepers mention this phenomenon in their writing. One person who does so is Robert Clyne, who refers to it in detail, identifying a storm petrel among the casualties.

This is an issue that has been raised on several occasions by the RSPB and other bodies, which led to the creation of bird-perches on some lighthouses in 1913. Questioning their effectiveness, it was raised again later, most notably by R M Lockley, the celebrated naturalist whose book *The Private Life of Rabbits* provided much of the inspiration for *Watership Down*, the novel by Richard Adams. In late 1936 he wrote an article in the *Daily Express* based on detailed observation and research in which he notes that a lighthouse's white flash blinds and confuses birds. (The same is not true, apparently, of a flashing red light.) Headlined 'The Storm Also Kills', he argues for 'a strong tray of stiff-wired netting, close-meshed … horizontally extended out from and surrounding the base of the lantern room'. By November 1956, when the issue is raised again by the RSPB, this idea seems to have been forgotten. Instead, there was the suggestion that if lighthouses were floodlit, this might go some way to solving the problem. Bell Rock lighthouse, however, has in fact taken the approach of fixing netting around its lamp to protect migrating birds while also protecting the light chamber from their fouling.

There is little doubt, however, that whatever measures might be taken, these seasonal routes have always been risk-laden and exhausting for the birds that undertook them, especially due to the existence of predators and the taxing nature of their journeys north or south. These dangers have increased over the course of the twentieth and twenty-first century, when many greater threats to the lives of birds than lighthouse towers have emerged, including the loss of their natural habitat and climate change. Among these has been the inexorable rise (and rise) of the skyscraper in cities both here and across the world. Bright lights entice the migrating birds in much the same way as they draw moths and other insects – a fatal attraction for birds which tower blocks and high-rise buildings can take to new and dizzy heights.

Yet rather than being neutral observers of phenomenon like this, it is apparent that many of those involved with the Northern Lighthouse Board are, like Eric Smith, the master of a number of Northern Lighthouse Board ships, enthralled with the wildlife they saw while they were at work. One of his favourite moments was sailing to Foula in the Shetland Isles, with its 370-metre cliffs, in the company of Princess Anne and seeing the sheer variety of seabirds

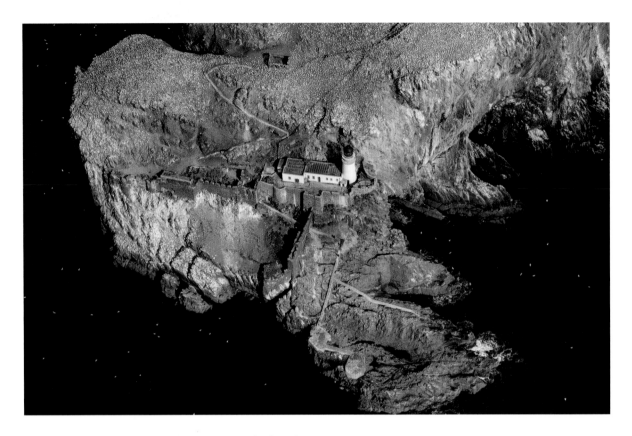

– the great skuas, arctic terns, kittiwakes – to be found there. He also pointed out the degree of care the organisation now displays towards the wildlife found around Scotland's coastline: Sulasgeir, Sule Skerry, Cape Wrath, Bass Rock, North Rona, Barra Head …

'These are just some of the places we avoid during the breeding season of the birds, in case we disturb them,' he informed me. 'Those in charge of our boats and helicopters spend ages taking note of all the regulations that are in place. There's individual policies and procedures on all our boats. We also make sure that any time we are in any location, we try to leave not a single imprint behind us, concealing where we've been, restoring the peat where we've made changes.'

This attention given to the environment by lightkeepers is not a new development. They have often played an important role in recording the natural life of this country. In some ways, they were encouraged in this by part of their job description – their responsibility for taking meteorological records every day. From 1868 onwards, they sent in reports of the weather, of wind, thunder, fog and even the occasional play and dance of the Northern Lights, the

Bass Rock Lighthouse

Serving as a hermitage for St Baldred in the seventh century, and as a prison hundreds of years later, Bass Rock's isolation and inaccessibility still inspire awe in those who see it today.
HES Canmore DP213998

aurora borealis, in the night sky. As Lawrence Tulloch notes in *On the Rocks*, this could be a complex task. Their detailed observations were carefully logged in a thick ledger that was not only designed to be used in weather forecasts but also for examining the climate and how it might alter and change. He writes that their observations would include:

> the amount of cloud and cloud types, wind speed and direction, barometer readings, temperature, and the temperature of a wet bulb so that the relative humidity could be recorded. Sea temperature was also taken once a day.

They even went so far as to calculate the 'dew-point' by 'using a slide rule'. It was a task that was often completed during the 2am to 6am watch, when all

was still and quiet and individuals were unlikely to be
disturbed.[6]

One of the phenomena lightkeepers did not expect
to record was the existence of earthquakes around the
Scottish coast. Yet this too occurred. On one occasion
in 1874, James Ewing, the principal keeper of Dubh
Artach, recorded how those within that building heard
a noise that 'resembled a booming of a cannon and
a tremendous motion was very apparent'. A similar
'strange rumbling noise' was also reported by the
principal keeper at Lismore on the morning of 23 April
1877. It 'made everything in the lighthouse shake at an
alarming rate'.

6 One story that Lawrence tells in his book is about his time in
Cape Wrath when he sent in rainfall readings that were questioned
by the Met Office in Wick. Their officials pointed out that, while
everyone else was informing them that the weather was dry, he
had reported that there had been several millimetres of rain on the
north-western edge of Sutherland. The mystery was solved when
a bearded collie, Brandy, owned by Principal Lightkeeper Donald
Macaulay – and brother of Calum who also appears in this book
– was observed to be raising his leg and urinating directly into the
rain gauge a few days later. After that, their rainfall reports were
more a matter of guesswork than exact recordings.

Yet, long before the official meteorological recording
of the nineteenth century, lightkeepers were engaged
and involved in the natural world. Lightkeepers even
attempted to preserve the great auk. A gaunt and
shrunken bird of this flightless variety was handed to
Robert Stevenson in 1821 by the lightkeeper on Eilean
Glas lighthouse in Scalpay, off the Isle of Harris. Some
natives of St Kilda had caught it three years previously.
Together with the Reverend Dr John Fleming,
who was professor of natural sciences at Edinburgh
University, the two men sought to keep the bird alive,
feeding it with fresh fish and allowing it occasionally
to dive and swim in the ocean with a cord fastened
onto its leg. It did this: 'with a rapidity that set all
pursuit from a boat with defiance'.

It is not clear how it happened, but sometime after
Fleming and Stevenson left the *Regent*, the Northern

Lighthouse Board yacht on which they travelled, the great auk made its escape near the entrance to the Firth of Clyde. Not long after that it was found washed ashore at Gourock, one of the last known of that species in these islands. One was later killed on Stac an Armin in St Kilda in July 1840, supposedly when the islanders mistook it for a witch that had just summoned up a storm. In worldwide terms, the final great auk, part of the long catalogue of animals and birds rendered extinct by mankind, was speared on the island of Eldey, 10 miles off the south-west coast of Iceland, on 3 July 1844. *Requiescat in pace.*

Lightkeepers also played an important role in charting the migratory routes of many of the birds that fly and swoop along our coastlines, often reporting these discoveries to men like the appropriately named W Eagle Clarke, a celebrated naturalist who completed his *Annals of Scottish Natural History*, published 1908, while working at the Edinburgh Museum of Science and Art – now the National Museum of Scotland. There were many individuals who did this while serving the Northern Lighthouse Board, men like James Tomison, Robert Wilson, Robert Agnew, J M Campbell (who wrote *Notes on the Natural History of the Bell Rock*, which was published in book form in 1904) and Robert Clyne. Originally from Kirriemuir in Angus, Clyne came from and extended a dynasty of lightkeepers. His brother John served at Kyleakin in Skye, Cape Wrath, St Abb's Head in Berwickshire, Noss Head in Caithness and various other postings. His daughter Lotte married a lightkeeper and her daughter married a crewman on the lighthouse supply vessels. It was as if each lighthouse beam transformed into its own distinct thread to create a patchwork of families – a not uncommon pattern in the households of lightkeepers the length and breadth of the country.

Clyne also was one of history's witnesses. In the last days of December 1879, he saw a great deal of tangled and broken wreckage float past the lighthouse on the Isle of May where he was on duty. A few

days later, he discovered this was some of the debris from the Tay Bridge Disaster, which took place on 28 December, the train crossing the bridge as it collapsed, plunging into the river below.

After leaving the Isle of May, Clyne worked at Langness lighthouse in the Isle of Man, at Rattray Head off Peterhead and at Bell Rock. Among the other locations he worked at was the one I saw from the kitchen window of my childhood home, the Butt of Lewis. He moved there in 1909. Despite finding the place rather 'bare and uninteresting' without much cover for small birds,[7] he took close and copious notes of the arrivals he glimpsed on the cliff-tops, noting in his first year at the station:

> The latter half of October has been exceptional, and I have been pleased to see a few warblers and other woodland birds about for the first time. On 25th and 26th we had blackcaps, redstarts and willow warblers. On 1st November I watched for a long time, catching midges on the cliff edge, what I am certain is a red-breasted flycatcher (*Muscipapa parva*), the same as I got last on the Bell Rock. The tail was nearly always on the move, and often erected wren-like, and the white feathers, when it made evolutions in the air, were as conspicuous as the white on the wheatear's rump.

I wonder what my ancestors would have thought of Robert Clyne if they saw him strolling around the lazy beds that are found not far away from the Butt of Lewis, making his way across the dunes of Eoropie beach. A keen photographer, he would often have had a camera dangling around his neck, a pen and notebook in his fingers. During the rare moments when he did not have a fishing rod in his grip, he was likely to be holding a home-made golf club, the parallel banks of ridge and furrow found within this landscape transformed – somewhat miraculously! – into the few holes of a golf course. For people with little concept of relaxation or leisure, he would have been a strange and startling character to encounter, even if they had some familiarity with his tongue.

St Abb's Head Lighthouse, Scottish Borders B Listed

A number of ships have been lost in this area, including the Royal Navy scout cruiser HMS *Pathfinder*, the first vessel to be destroyed by a self-propelled torpedo. This incident took place on 5 September 1914 with the loss of 259 lives, following an attack by a German U-boat.

HES Canmore DP062457

7 He bemoans the lack of turnips in the area. His words might have influenced people. I recall fields filled with the crop, which both I – and the other village boys – used to regularly raid, clambering over fences to steal them.

He writes articulately about his trade, describing it in the following terms:

> Seldom is there the chance of diversions that fall to the ordinary. The lightkeeper's cinema is a sky screen, when the dramas, and the damsel in distress is some frail barque with as pretty a name as ever fiction heroine had.

The average Lewisman of that time would have been puzzled by such comparisons – concepts such as 'cinemas' and 'screens' alien to his existence. In a different way, previous generations living on the edge of Scotland would have been bewildered by some of the ways of thinking that are associated with lighthouses today. Davie Ferguson, who works at Ardnamurchan, told me about some of the activities at the lighthouse there. It stands on the most westerly point of the Scottish mainland, at the far end of 26 miles of single-track road which seem to grow increasingly narrow and twisted the closer a driver gets to the tower. This, as I discovered on the one occasion I travelled in its direction, seems to heighten and emphasise the distance. Each turn and pause in the road stretches out the time spent upon it, making me long to acquire the whoosh and wings of the occasional bird of prey – perhaps buzzard, eagle or sea-eagle – that passed over the roof of the car.

'It's a long, long peninsula,' Davie declares. He maintains, however, that both the destination and surroundings make the effort worthwhile. The buildings contain a museum, called – appropriately enough – Kingdom of Light or Rioghachd na Sorcha. When the lighthouse was constructed by Alan Stevenson and his team in 1849, he (in line with the architectural fashion of the time) made it into the most 'Egyptian' of all that family's creations, with Egyptian figurines, among other features, ornamenting the lamp base.[8]

It's as if one of the Time Lords from *Dr Who* had been transported to the location, giving the tower the benefit of the decorations that once adorned the Pharos lighthouse before it tumbled into the sea.

It is both at its foot and the gallery of the lighthouse that people stand when they visit during the summer, taking part in the Whale Trail that links locations in the Scottish mainland and the Inner and Outer Hebrides – with plans to extend to the Northern Isles. These sites include lighthouses like Tiumpan Head in Lewis, Eilean Glas in Harris, the former lightkeepers' quarters in Hynish in Tiree, the communities of Tobermory, Staffin and Gairloch, tourist highlights such as Duart Castle in Mull and the beach that doubles as an airport in Barra. Rather than being engaged in the whirl of modern tourism, visiting one location after another, this encourages visitors to spend some time standing and staring, pausing and taking note of their surroundings. Organised by the Hebridean Whale and Dolphin Trust, this form of 'slow-tourism' is designed to make visitors gape and draw breath at the numerous whales and dolphins found within the stretch of the Minch; their observations assisted by the team of volunteers who stand alongside them, their fingers pointing out the tell-tale signs of tail and fin, a small disturbance in a wave.

Again, they make me think of my own ancestors, to whom such sights were almost commonplace, who only lifted their heads to look at the horizon when something infinitely more unusual and dramatic had occurred.

Perhaps a ship rising and falling on waves that in size and scale imitate the faces of the cliff which they strike …

Perhaps the Commissioners arriving on their vessel to inspect the local lighthouse …

Perhaps the sight of an emigrant vessel taking the people of their own community away from their native shores.

---

8 There are a few competitors for that title. Alan Stevenson's love of both academia and Egypt can be seen in several of his creations. At Covesea Skerries, near Lossiemouth, the lantern rests on long, Egyptian-style stone arches. Classical Greece also influences the pedestal on which a lens sits while the face of one of the Greek goddesses decorates the brass air vents. In Noss Head, near Wick, the lightkeepers' cottages are designed in an Egyptian style.

Ardnamurchan Lighthouse, Highland A Listed

At the end of a long road, this 36-metre tower looks out towards the sights and scenes of the Inner Hebrides. Nearby, there are the former keepers' cottages and outbuildings, managed by the Ardnamurchan Lighthouse Trust since 1996.

HES Canmore DP139215

Conclusion
Embers

Inside my wine bottle
I was constructing a lighthouse
While all the others
Were making sailing ships.

Charles Simic, 'Solving the Riddle',
Selected Poems, 1963–1983

It is not often a village landmark performs a
vanishing trick.

Yet this is precisely what was done by a cairn of
stones standing within the Aird Dell fence in my
native Ness in the Isle of Lewis a few years ago.
Called Càrn an Cailean by locals, it stood on the
edge of tiny Loch Sgreuchabhat for nearly a hundred
years only to disappear from that area of improved
common grazing one particular day or night.

It was a cairn I sometimes stood beside when,
together with others of my age-group, we wandered
in that direction. Our fingers would rub against the
layer of moss that seemed to have formed its own fur
on the cairn, nails picking at the orange lichen that

Rattray Head Lighthouse, Aberdeenshire B Listed
Accessible by means of a wide causeway that is just about visible
by low tide, the necessity of this building can be seen in the
wreckage found close to hand. According to a report by engineer
David Alan Stevenson, the area 'was notorious among mariners
for its foul ground, rapid tides and high and dangerous seas. No
part of the East Coast of Scotland was more dangerous than this.'
Ian Cowe

clustered like small flowers on the rock. On bleak days,
they resembled tiny suns bringing their own glimpses
of light to the landscape.

It was the cairn itself, however, that provoked the
most wonder. Some stones seemed precariously in
place, large slabs of rock balancing on the ledges of
those that had been lifted there before. As I wondered
for a moment about how they defied gravity, I might
have placed my own small pebbles on its summit; my
own tiny contribution to – what appeared to me – a
timeless stack of Lewisian gneiss. Built in an age before
machinery, its construction clearly involved a great
deal of grit, effort and strength. Those who made the
cairn must have heaved and sweated as they shoved
each stone into place, ensuring it stayed upright,
making certain that the last one they hauled up would
not topple or dislodge the rest. By some miracle, they
managed to achieve this, their monument of rock
remaining upright for 90 or so years through all the
winds and storms that harassed and bullied this bare
edge of land.

It was my neighbour, Donald Macleod (or
Domhnall Aost), who told me the story of its creation,
how several young men from South Dell had gone
out there to erect this cairn of stone beside Loch
Sgreuchabhat. It was an act performed in the hours
before they travelled to Stornoway the following
morning to take the ship the *Metagama* to Saint John,
New Brunswick, in Canada, emigrating forever to a
new land out west. It was a task, too, that was done to
honour a tradition even older than the lighthouse on

Rudha Robhanais or the Butt of Lewis not far away. At one time, people left similar structures standing at various points not just on the shoreline but also on the moor, enabling them to find their way home if fog, snow and storm made their usual destinations look strange and unfamiliar, rendering them lost and disorientated.

Leaving their homes for the last time on 25 April 1923, it is easy to picture these young men that night. They must have trembled as much from the threat of tears as they did from the burden of the rocks they were carrying, gulping back sighs and sorrows as they thought of how they would never step on this edge of the village again. Over the course of the following days, a bonfire was lit alongside the cairn – one last signal from those remaining on the island to the *Metagama* as it neared the Butt on its voyage. It was the village's own lighthouse, a temporary blaze of heat and light, similar to those that villagers had lit when local men were at sea years before the Butt had come into existence. It cast its glow on local landmarks – the glen they called Dibadale, Sgeir Dhail or Dell Rock, Dùn Arnaistean near the village beach – not lost or submerged in the beam cast upon other villages to the north, but distinctive and clear on their own land. It acted too as a reminder of words within the Bible, Jeremiah 31: 21, with its injunction to:

> set up signposts,
> make landmarks;
> set your heart toward the highway,
> the way in which you went.

At some time over recent years, this waymark with its connection to the 'way in which we went' was lost, disappearing from the landscape in hours of darkness or light. Yet it is difficult for me to condemn too harshly those that performed this vanishing trick. Like me, as a young man in the village, they probably never knew the story of the boys from Dell who built that pedestal of stone nor imagined the bonfire that once flamed by its side. They may have needed the rocks for perfectly good reasons – to form part of the foundation for a barn or house, to become a small section of wall – and they decided to do what was both quick and convenient, loading their weight into the back of a trailer and trundling down the road to some undisclosed location.

In doing this, however, they were guilty of a small offence. Anyone glimpsing these stones with their coat of lichen and moss, their place at the edge of a loch, should have been conscious that they were of some significance. They did not appear there intact and whole overnight. In removing them from their place, these people accidentally broke faith with those who lived on the island in the past, especially those who left its shores decades ago for the farms of Ontario and Manitoba, the cities of Toronto and Detroit. They tore down that memory and left only a ghost in its place.

But what about the survival of Scotland's other vital waymarks, its lighthouses? Over the last few decades, there have been a succession of measures introduced to improve the safety of ships at sea. There are, for instance, established procedures to follow if vessels encounter problems. They can radio through a Mayday call to the shore. The coastguard will then decide what measures to take, whether to send out a lifeboat or helicopter or even if to inform other boats nearby of what is happening and ask them to assist the vessel in trouble. In addition, there are developments like GMDSS – the Global Maritime Distress and Safety System – which deals with what happens when a vessel is in distress. This is linked to the Global Positioning System or GPS, one of a number of developments by which we know exactly where we are positioned in this world.

Yet thankfully there is still good reason for the existence of lighthouses around our coasts. Most good seamen do not rely solely on technology, and heed the warning that the presence of a lighthouse represents. As Ruaraidh Macrae, one of those who now helps to maintain the lighthouses of Lewis and Harris, pointed out to me, they still know how to chart their course and progress on a map. They are aware exactly which lighthouse is in their vicinity, able to recognise the character of the light that flashes in their direction, whether it might be Sumburgh Head or Muckle Flugga. People still need to know where they are – like those who sought to spot the coastline of South Dell when they emigrated to Canada. It is a human comfort to know there are others in existence out on the horizon. With so many lighthouses protected, their significance recorded by their listed building status, they will continue to be landmarks – whether viewed from sea or land. In that role, the last decades have made lighthouses even more important than they used to be, especially when located in our coastal towns. The landscape has altered considerably and one may no longer find the silhouettes and outlines that made

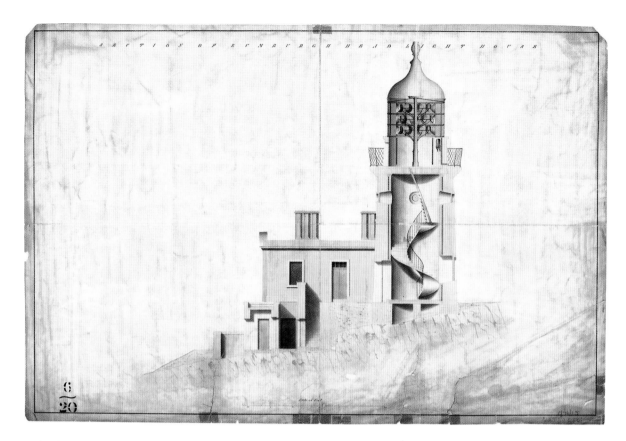

each of our settlements distinctive and different – lighthouses remain a unique beacon, whether their lights still shine or not.

And something else will be lost if we learn to depend too much on the insights that technology provides. We will stop 'seeing' places, either by compass or map or indeed in the inner workings of our mind. Way back in the 1940s, a psychologist called Edward Tolman who worked in the University of California put forward the idea that many animals possess a 'cognitive map' that enables them to find their way around the world. It is found within us – and the migrating birds that occasionally dash themselves against man-made lights – in the hippocampus, a seahorse-shaped structure found deep inside our medial temporal lobe.[1] In both buzzard and boy, gull and girl, this tiny tissue stores our maps and memories. In fact, the two are bound together. Our memories of a location help us remember. So do the stories we tell about a place. As such, there is more than a little truth

1 This finding was discovered by the anatomist John O'Keefe, who won the Nobel Prize in 2014.

Sumburgh Head Lighthouse, Shetland A Listed
'It is proposed to have a light on Sumburgh-head, which is the first land made by vessels coming from the eastward; Fitful-head is higher, but it is to the west, from which quarter few vessels come,' wrote Sir Walter Scott in his journal in 1814. This elegant drawing offers an insight into the structure planned for the headland overlooking a stretch of sea where two tidal streams meet with often dramatic results.
c1820 drawing. NLB Canmore DP352563

in Jeanette Winterson's observation that people see lighthouses and the places they stand in terms of the stories they generate. I will forever remember Pladda lighthouse because of an aside Ian Duff told me about the lobster creels they used to place in the waters there. Each time I hear the words 'Pentland Skerries', I will think of Calum MacArthur's stories and how he used to occupy his time putting ships into bottles during his hours off duty on that island. And then there are Jonathan Wills' stories of Muckle Flugga, how the workforce building new accommodation for the lightkeepers erected goalposts – complete with crossbar – on nearby Tipta Skerry.

Holy Isle (Inner) Lighthouse, Arran

Known locally as 'Wee Donald', this lighthouse, built in 1877, faces the east coast of the Isle of Arran at the south entrance to Lamlash Bay.

HES Canmore DP221548

During a recent summer, I spent a week or so in Arran, staying in the Scottish School of Herbal Medicine in Kildonan. I looked out at the island of Pladda with its two lighthouses of different sizes, one large, the other some 20 feet lower, before me, pondering too the outline of Ailsa Craig, seemingly only the sweep of a curling stone away when the sea was unruffled and calm. Uneven stepping stones on the way to Ireland, they appeared an ill-matched pair – the first flat and in close proximity to Arran, keeping a wave- and weather-watch over a narrow channel, a bald sea with barely a twist or curl of water; the other sharp and well-defined, a monolith with its own lighthouse anchored on a ledge of rock, its size and scale dominating even on the days that storms pummelled this coastline. Looking out at these towers, both on Pladda and Ailsa Craig, there is no doubt that there were mornings

when the structures seemed a surreal and theatrical sight. One or two of our group kept glancing in their direction, as if they feared that these buildings would be snatched away, stolen from the dream in which they lived for a short time.

This feeling was probably made more intense a short time later, when, as a group, we arrived on Holy Isle, taking the boat across the narrow stretch of water from Arran. Accompanied by the others, I stepped into a space that, in a Scottish context, seemed distant and extraordinary. The path towards the building known as

Holy Isle (Outer) Lighthouse, Arran

The Northern Lighthouse Board's first square lighthouse, also known as Pillar Rock, the place on which it stands. The island is owned by the Samye Ling Buddhist community.

Ian Cowe

the Centre for World Peace and Health was festooned with Tibetan prayer flags and ceremonial mounds known as stupas, where people were supposed to bow heads and grant homage. The garden next door was decorated with fairy figures, creatures of myth and legend. This was all part of an environment fashioned and shaped by a group of Tibetan Buddhist monks who had arrived on the island a few decades earlier after many in that country had been involved in the uprising against Chinese rule in 1959. They offered courses in yoga, tai chi and mindfulness within their

walls, seeking to grant peace to others in a place where they enjoyed safety and security, the comfort of no longer being persecuted for their faith.

There were other ways in which we stepped out of time and place that day. Under the shelter of Mullach Mor, the 'big top' or mountain that dominates Holy Isle, we come across one or two of the Eriskay ponies that are allowed to roam free across the island. A flock of that ancient breed of sheep, the Soay, rests on the foreshore, chewing the dark layers of kelp and bladderwrack the tide has washed up on the shore. Birds of prey hover – like both they and the hour of the clock have been suspended. Even the roll of the ocean seems to have stilled for the day.

Some of our group make our way further along the shoreline, trying to find sight of the cave where an ancient Celtic saint, Molaise, was reputed to have once lived (giving his name too to the village of Lamlash, a word derived from the Gaelic Eilean Molaise (Molaise island) and transformed and altered over the course of years). We fail to spot this, identifying various slashes in rock or slope where he might have cowered in shelter, but nothing that could be identified with either confidence or certainty.

Apart from one thing. In front of us, there stood a lighthouse, Holy Isle Outer or Pillar Rock Light. Built in 1905, it was the Northern Lighthouse Board's first square tower, distinct and odd in its shape and structure, a companion to its older neighbour, Holy Isle Inner constructed nearly 30 years earlier. Nowadays, the dwellings around it have become – what its creator, David Alan Stevenson,

could never have imagined they would ever be – a refuge for an order of Buddhist nuns who live there in seclusion and retreat for a period of three years. One can only imagine how the fervour of their worship travels through the air around Holy Isle, the memories of prayers uttered by St Molaise who gave the island its Gaelic name mingling with those of the Buddhist monks and nuns who now live on Holy Isle, the sound of their words pulsing like the lighthouse beam.

Let their voices ring out, ensuring their words are proclaimed not just for thanksgiving and homage, but – just as importantly – 'for the safety of all'.

Let them shine.

Appendix
Designated Lighthouses

Lighthouses and closely related structures
that have been Listed and Scheduled by
Historic Environment Scotland

Visit portal.historicenvironment.scot to find out more

Aberdeen Harbour Leading Lights
Aberdeen
B Listed – 2019 (LB52520)

Ailsa Craig Lighthouse
South Ayrshire
B Listed – 1977 (LB1151)

Ardnamurchan Lighthouse
Highland
A Listed – 1971 (LB521)

Ardrishaig Harbour
Argyll & Bute
B Listed – 1971 (LB18252)

Arnish Lighthouse
Na h-Eileanan Siar
B Listed – 1971 (LB13328)

Auskerry Lighthouse
Orkney
B Listed – 1971 (LB18638)

Ayr Harbour
South Ayrshire
B Listed – 1971 (LB21592)

Barns Ness Lighthouse
East Lothian
B Listed – 1986 (LB1465)

Barra Head Lighthouse
Na h-Eileanan Siar
A Listed – 1971 (LB5893)

Bass Rock Lighthouse
East Lothian
C Listed – 1989 (LB14738)

Bell Rock Lighthouse
Angus
A Listed – 1998 (LB45197)

Bell Rock Lighthouse Signal Tower
Angus
A Listed – 1971 (LB21230)

Berriedale Navigation Beacons
Highland
B Listed – 1984 (LB7931)

Black's Memorial Lighthouse
Argyll & Bute
B Listed – 2020 (LB52560)

Bound Skerry Lighthouse
Shetland
B Listed – 1971 (LB19894)

Breasclete, Lighthouse Keepers' Houses
Na h-Eileanan Siar
B Listed – 1993 (LB18655)

Bressay Lighthouse
Shetland
B Listed – 1977 (LB5882)

Buchan Ness Lighthouse
Aberdeenshire
A Listed – 1971 (LB16367)

Buckie Harbour Leading Light
Moray
C Listed – 1989 (LB22722)

Buckie Harbour Lighthouse
Moray
C Listed – 1989 (LB22724)

Buddon Ness (High) Lighthouse
Angus
B Listed – 1971 (LB4634)

Buddon Ness (Low) Lighthouse
Angus
B Listed –1971 (LB4635)

Buddon Ness (Old) Lighthouse
Angus
C Listed – 1980 (LB4633)

Burghead Harbour
Moray
B Listed – 1974 (LB22749)

Bound Skerry Lighthouse B Listed

HES Canmore DP146027

Buchan Ness Lighthouse A Listed

NLB Canmore DP070822

Burnmouth Harbour
Scottish Borders
B Listed – 1999 (LB11)

Burrafirth, Muckle Flugga Lighthouse Shore Station
Shetland
C Listed – 1998 (LB45291)

Butt Of Lewis Lighthouse
Na h-Eileanan Siar
A Listed –1971 (LB5768)

Caledonian Canal, Bona Lighthouse
Highland
B Listed – 1971

Caledonian Canal, Corpach Locks and Basin
Highland
Scheduled Monument – 1992 (SM5297)

Caledonian Canal, Fort Augustus to Loch Ness
Highland
Scheduled Monument – 1975 (SM3614)

Caledonian Canal, Gairlochy Locks, Lighthouse and Signal Lamp
Highland
Scheduled Monument – 1992 (SM5294)

Calvay Lighthouse, Taigh-solais Chalbhaigh
Na h-Eileanan Siar
C Listed – 2020 (LB52572)

Cantick Head Lighthouse
Orkney
B Listed –1971 (LB18710)

Cape Wrath Lighthouse
Highland
A Listed – 1971 (LB488)

Cape Wrath, Lloyd's Signal Station
Highland
B Listed – 2013 (LB52037)

Chanonry Point Lighthouse
Highland
A Listed –1971 (LB31799)

Cloch Lighthouse
Inverclyde
B Listed – 1971 (LB13820)

Copinsay Lighthouse
Orkney
B Listed – 1971 (LB18574)

Corran Point Lighthouse
Highland
C Listed – 1971 (LB1689)

Corran Point Lighthouse, Store
Highland
C Listed – 1985 (LB1691)

**Corran Point, Tigh Soluis
(Former Lighthouse Keepers' Dwellings)**
Highland
C Listed – 1985 (LB1690)

Corsewall Lighthouse
Dumfries & Galloway
A Listed – 1972 (LB9923)

Covesea Skerries Lighthouse
Moray
A Listed – 1971 (LB37605)

Cromarty Lighthouse
Highland
A Listed – 1971 (LB23680)

Cullen Harbour and Harbour Light
Moray
B Listed – 1972 (LB23803)

Davaar Lighthouse
Argyll & Bute
B Listed – 1980 (LB4920)

Dennis Head, Old Beacon
Orkney
Scheduled Monument – 1997 (SM6596)

Dubh Artach Lighthouse
Argyll & Bute
A Listed – 1971 (LB12320)

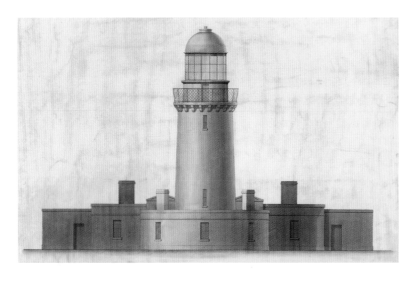

Dunnet Head Lighthouse B Listed
NLB Canmore DP005830

Eilean Glas Lighthouse A Listed
HES Canmore DP235428

Fair Isle (North) Lighthouse B Listed
HES Canmore DP259998

Dunnet Head Lighthouse
Highland
B Listed – 1984 (LB1890)

Dunollie Lighthouse
Argyll & Bute
C Listed – 2020 (LB52570)

Dunure Harbour
South Ayrshire
B Listed – 1971 (LB19683)

East Lighthouse, Tayport
Fife
B Listed –1973 (LB41950)

East Vows Beacon
Fife
B Listed – 2020 (LB52567)

Eilean A' Chùirn Lighthouse
Argyll & Bute
C Listed – 2020 (LB52574)

Eilean Glas Lighthouse
Na h-Eileanan Siar
A Listed – 1994 (LB13487)

Elie Ness Lighthouse
Fife
C Listed – 1980 (LB8997)

Erraid Shore Station (Observatory)
Argyll & Bute
C Listed – 1980 (LB12309)

Esha Ness Lighthouse
Shetland
B Listed – 1997 (LB44556)

Fair Isle (North) Lighthouse
Shetland
B Listed – 1977 (LB5446)

Fair Isle (South) Lighthouse
Shetland
B Listed – 1977 (LB5411)

Fair Isle Rocket Signalling Establishment
Shetland
Scheduled Monument – 1996 (SM6583)

Fidra Lighthouse
East Lothian
C Listed – 1971 (LB1336)

Fife Ness Lighthouse
Fife
B Listed – 2020 (LB52557)

Firths Voe (Mossbank) Lighthouse
Shetland
C Listed – 1997 (LB44532)

Fladda Lighthouse
Argyll & Bute
B Listed – 1971 (LB11588)

Flannan Isles Lighthouse
Na h-Eileanan Siar
B Listed – 2001 (LB48143)

Gallanach Road Lighthouse Depot
Argyll & Bute
C Listed – 2003 (LB49357)

Gasay Lighthouse, Taigh-solais Ghasaigh
Na h-Eileanan Siar
C Listed – 2020 (LB52576)

Girdle Ness Lighthouse
Aberdeen
A Listed – 1967 (LB20078)

Gourdon Harbour Leading Light
Aberdeenshire
C Listed – 2013 (LB52082)

Granton Harbour, Mid Pier Leading Light
Edinburgh
B Listed – 1989 (LB30218)

Greenock Esplanade, Cast-Iron Navigation Light
Inverclyde
B Listed – 1990 (LB34179)

Holborn Head Lighthouse B Listed
HES Canmore SC903113

Inchkeith Lighthouse B Listed
HES Canmore DP055885

Killantringan Lighthouse B Listed
HES 008-000-012-766-R

Grutness, Lighthouse Store
Shetland
C Listed – 1997 (LB44543)

Halliman Skerries Beacon
Moray
B Listed – 2020 (LB52566)

Hawes Pier Lighthouse
Edinburgh
B Listed – 1971 (LB40353)

Holborn Head Lighthouse
Highland
B Listed – 1984 (LB14952)

Hoy Sound (High) Lighthouse
Orkney
A Listed –1977 (LB12736)

Hoy Sound (Low) Lighthouse
Orkney
B Listed – 1977 (LB13841)

Hynish Shore Station
Argyll & Bute
A Listed – 1971 (LB17848)

Inchkeith Lighthouse
Fife
B Listed – 1971 (LB9707)

Island of Rona Lighthouse
Highland
B Listed – 1971 (LB18449)

Isle of May, Fluke Street
Fife
B Listed – 1984 (LB2713)

Isle of May Lighthouse
Fife
B Listed – 1984 (LB2712)

Isle of May Low Light
Fife
C Listed – 1984 (LB2687)

Isle of May North Horn
Fife
C Listed – 1984 (LB2688)

Isle of May South Horn
Fife
C Listed – 1984 (LB2689)

Isle of May, The Beacon, Former Lighthouse
Fife
Scheduled Monument – 1958 (SM887)

Isle Ornsay Lighthouse
Highland
B Listed – 1982 (LB14008)

Kilkerran Cottage
Argyll & Bute
C Listed – 1980 (LB22961)

Killantringan Lighthouse
Dumfries & Galloway
B Listed – 1972 (LB16758)

Kinnaird Head Lighthouse
Aberdeenshire
A Listed – 1971 (LB31888)

Kirkwall Harbour Light (Old)
Orkney
C Listed – 2008 (LB51038)

Kyleakin Lighthouse
Highland
B Listed – 1971 (LB6994)

Lady Isle Lighthouse and Navigational Beacon
South Ayrshire
B Listed – 2020 (LB52564)

Lismore Lighthouse, Eilean Musdile
Argyll & Bute
A Listed – 1971 (LB12360)

Little Cumbrae Lighthouse
North Ayrshire
Scheduled Monument – 1957 (SM418)

Little Cumbrae (New Lighthouse)
North Ayrshire
B Listed – 1971 (LB852)

Little Ross Lighthouse
Dumfries & Galloway
B Listed – 1971 (LB3399)

Loch Ryan Lighthouse
Dumfries & Galloway
B Listed – 1972 (LB10169)

Lybster Harbour
Highland
B Listed – 1984 (LB7954)

Melvin House Beacon
Orkney
B Listed – 1998 (LB45398)

Monach Lighthouse
Na h-Eileanan Siar
B Listed – 1971 (LB17578)

Montrose Harbour Inner Light
Angus
B Listed – 1999 (LB38223)

Muckle Flugga Lighthouse
Shetland
A Listed – 1971 (LB17479)

Mull of Galloway, East Tarbet, Cottage and Quay
Dumfries & Galloway
B Listed – 1994 (LB10126)

Mull of Galloway Lighthouse
Dumfries & Galloway
A Listed – 1972 (LB13578)

Mull of Kintyre Lighthouse
Argyll & Bute
A Listed – 1971 (LB19874)

Neist Point Lighthouse
Highland
B Listed – 1971 (LB465)

Newhaven, New Lighthouse
Edinburgh
B Listed – 1970 (LB43712)

Newhaven, Old Harbour Light
Edinburgh
B Listed – 1970 (LB43713)

North Carr Beacon
Fife
B Listed – 2020 (LB52556)

North Carr Beacon Construction Site
Fife
Scheduled Monument – 2020 (SM13733)

North Queensferry, Pierhead, Lantern Tower
Fife
A Listed – 1979 (LB9998)

North Queensferry, Town Pier
Fife
A Listed – 1973 (LB9978)

North Ronaldsay Lighthouse
Orkney
B Listed – 1971 (LB5892)

Northern Lighthouse Board Offices, 84 George Street
Edinburgh
A Listed – 1966 (LB28877)

Northern Lighthouse and Buoy Depot
Edinburgh
C Listed – 1998 (LB45659)

Northern Lighthouse Board Engineering, Storage and Testing Facility
Edinburgh
C Listed – 1985 (LB29925)

Northern Lighthouse Board Depot Managers House, 'The Haven'
Orkney
B Listed – 1971 (LB41835)

Mull of Galloway Lighthouse **A Listed**
HES 008-000-012-957-R

Oxcars Lighthouse B Listed
HES Canmore DP0077619

Port Glasgow Harbour Lighthouse
B Listed
HES Canmore SC682389

Rhinns of Islay Lighthouse A Listed
HES Canmore DP309288

Noss Head Lighthouse
Highland
A Listed – 1984 (LB14087)

Noup Head Lighthouse
Orkney
B Listed – 1971 (LB18736)

Outskerries Lighthouse Keeper's Houses
Shetland
C Listed – 1998 (LB45283)

Oxcars Lighthouse
Fife
B Listed – 2004 (LB49687)

Pentland Skerries Lighthouses
Orkney
A Listed – 1971 (LB18728)

Pile Lighthouse, Tayport
Fife
B Listed – 1973 (LB9009)

Port Ellen Lighthouse
Argyll & Bute
B Listed – 1971 (LB11973)

Port Glasgow Harbour, Leading Light
Inverclyde
B Listed – 1990 (LB40085)

Port Glasgow Harbour Lighthouse
Inverclyde
B Listed – 1990 (LB40086)

Port Logan Lighthouse
Dumfries & Galloway
B Listed – 1972 (LB13586)

Portpatrick Harbour
Dumfries & Galloway
B Listed – 1979 (LB16776)

Rattray Head Lighthouse
Aberdeenshire
B Listed – 1971 (LB3042)

Rhinns of Islay Lighthouse
Argyll & Bute
A Listed – 1971 (LB11944)

Rhuvaal Lighthouse
Argyll & Bute
B Listed – 1971 (LB12117)

Rose Ness Lighthouse
Orkney
C Listed – 2020 (LB52571)

Rosehearty Harbour
Aberdeenshire
B Listed – 1971 (LB40433)

Ruadh Sgeir Lighthouse
Argyll & Bute
C Listed – 2020 (LB52575)

Rubha nan Gall Lighthouse
Argyll & Bute
C Listed – 1980 (LB11015)

Rubha Reidh Lighthouse
Highland
B Listed – 2004 (LB49894)

Ruvha'an Eun Minor Light
Argyll & Bute
C Listed – 1998 (LB44998)

Sanda Lighthouse
Argyll & Bute
A Listed – 2020 (LB52565)

Scurdie Ness Lighthouse (Montroseness Lighthouse)
Angus
B Listed – 1971 (LB4958)

Scurdie Ness, East Beacon and West Beacon
Angus
B Listed – 1971 (LB4959)

Shapinsay Lighthouse
Orkney
B Listed – 1977 (LB18619)

Skerryvore Lighthouse
Argyll & Bute
A Listed – 1971 (LB17849)

Southerness Lighthouse
Dumfries & Galloway
A Listed – 1971 (LB10415)

St Abb's Head Lighthouse
Scottish Borders
B Listed – 1971 (LB4103)

St Abb's Head, Lightkeeper's Cottage
Scottish Borders
C Listed – 2000 (LB46662)

Start Point Lighthouse
Orkney
B Listed – 1971 (LB12675)

Stoer Head Lighthouse
Highland
B Listed – 1979 (LB1833)

Sule Skerry Lighthouse
Orkney
A Listed – 1971 (LB18598)

Sule Skerry Lighthouse Station
Orkney
C Listed – 1998 (LB45408)

Sumburgh Head Lighthouse
Shetland
A Listed – 1977 (LB5442)

Tarbat Ness Lighthouse
Highland
A Listed – 1971 (LB14100)

Telford Beacon, Dundee Waterfront near Tay Bridge
Dundee
C Listed – 1989 (LB24966)

The Riv Beacon
Orkney
B Listed – 2020 (LB52568)

Tiumpan Head Lighthouse
Na h-Eileanan Siar
C Listed – 1971 (LB19209)

Todhead Lighthouse
Aberdeenshire
B Listed – 1972 (LB9535)

Toward Lighthouse
Argyll & Bute
B Listed – 1980 (LB5070)

Troon Harbour
South Ayrshire
B Listed – 1998 (LB45262)

Turnberry Lighthouse
South Ayrshire
B Listed – 1992 (LB12991)

Ve Skerries Lighthouse
Shetland
B Listed – 2020 (LB52569)

West Lighthouse, Tayport
Fife
B Listed – 1973 (LB41953)

Wick Harbour Lighthouses
Highland
B Listed – 1984 (LB42309)

Start Point Lighthouse B Listed

Ian Cowe

Tarbat Ness Lighthouse A Listed

HES Canmore DP042273

Turnberry Lighthouse B Listed

HES Canmore DP050322

Bibliography

Non-Fiction

The Genius of Birds
Jennifer Ackerman (Corsair, 2016)

Shipwrecks of the North of Scotland
R N Baird (Birlinn, 2003)

The Lighthouse Stevensons
Bella Bathurst (Harper Perennial, 1999)

The Wreckers
Bella Bathurst (Harper, 2005)

On Lighthouses
Jazmina Barrera, translated by Christina MacSweeney
(Two Lines Press, 2020)

*An Tuil – The Flood: Anthology of 20th-Century Scottish
Gaelic Verse* Edited by Ronald Black (Polygon, 1999)

Scottish and Manx Lighthouses
Ian Cowe (Northern Lighthouse Heritage Trust, 2018)

The Scottish Clearances: A History of the Dispossessed
T M Devine (Penguin, 2018)

Hebridean Sharker
Tex Geddes (Herbert Jenkins Ltd, 1960)

A Maritime History of Scotland 1650–1790
Eric J Graham (John Donald, 2015)

Sentinels of the Sea
R G Grant (Thames and Hudson, National Archives, 2018)

Stargazing: Memoirs of a Young Lighthouse Keeper
Peter Hill (Canongate, 2003)

Scotland's Lighthouses in Photographs by John Hume
John Hume (Stenlake Publishing, 2020)

Shipwreck Index of the British Isles: Scotland
Richard and Bridget Larn (Lloyds, 1998)

The Island Lighthouses of Scotland
John A Love (Island Book Trust, 2011)

A Natural History of Lighthouses
John A Love (Whittles, 2015)

Scottish Lighthouse Pioneers
Paul A Lynn (Whittles, 2017)

Archie's Lights
Archie MacEachern and Anne MacEachern (Whittles, 2019)

Wonder Tales from Scottish Myth and Legend
Donald Alexander Mackenzie (Blackie and Son, 1917)

A Star for Seaman
Craig Mair (John Murray, 1978)

Northern Lights: The Age of Scottish Lighthouses
A D Morrison-Low (National Museums Scotland, 2010)

The Wreck of the Annie Jane
Allan F Murray (Acair, 2017)

Seashaken Houses
Tom Nancollas (Particular Books, 2018)

Lighthouse
Tony Parker (Eland, 1975)

Bell Rock Lighthouse: An Illustrated History
Michael A W Strachan (Amberley, 2016)

Scottish Lighthouses: An Illustrated History
Michael A W Strachan (Amberley, 2016)

On the Rocks: A Lightkeeper's Tale
Lawrence Tulloch (Shetland Times, 2009)

Fiction

The Lighthouse Keeper's Lunch
Ronda and David Armitage (Scholastic, 2017)

'The Foghorn' in *The Golden Apples of the Sun*
Ray Bradbury (Harper Perennials, 1997)

'The Lighthouse' in *Agnes Owens: The Complete Short Stories*
Agnes Owens (Polygon, 2008)

Pharos
Alice Thompson (Virago Press, 2002)

Lighthousekeeping
Jeanette Winterson (Fourth Estate, 2004)

To the Lighthouse
Virginia Woolf (Wordsworth, 1994)

Poetry

Anne Stevenson in *The Oxford Book of The Sea*
Jonathan Raban (Oxford University Press 1992)

Newspaper and Journal Articles

Lockley, R M 'The Storm Also Kills'
(*Daily Express*, 15 December 1936)

Rodríguez, Airam *et al* 'Seabird mortality induced by
land-based artificial lights.'
(*Conservation Biology vol. 31,5* 2017 986–1001)

Wills, Jonathan 'Muckle Flugga and Me'
(*Shetland Life*, 9 January and 6 February 2009)

Worthington, David 'Ferries in The Firthlands:
Communications, Society and Culture Along a Northern
Scottish Rural Coast c1600–c1809'
(*Rural History*, 14 September 2016)

Websites

Northern Lighthouse Board:
www.nlb.org.uk/lighthouses/

HES Designations portal:
portal.historicenvironment.scot/

HES Canmore:
canmore.org.uk/

Acknowledgements

The writing of books can often be a lonely enterprise. As a result, it is important to acknowledge the other human beings who make it possible, contributing to the venture in a hundred different ways, from providing necessary pieces of information to moments of human comfort. Many of those who supplied the former are named in the pages of this book. They are people like Helen Moncrieff, Peter Johnson, Brian Johnson, J J Jamieson, Calum Macaulay, Eric Smith, Jonathan Wills, Ian Duff, Aine Stapleton, Lynda McGuigan, Michael Strachan, Michael Cruickshank, Donald John Smith, Karen Clarke, Davie Ferguson, Ruaraidh Macrae, Angus Smith, Chris Barratt, Professor John R Hume and others.

However, they are outnumbered by those who provided help and are not named in this book. They include those like Chris Dyer and Eileen Brooke-Freeman, who are employed by the Shetland Amenity Trust and gave me information about Sumburgh Head; my old friend Iain Gordon Macdonald, Annie MacSween and Comunn Eachdraidh Nis, who supplied similar material about the Butt of Lewis; Karen Fraser and the staff of Shetland Library; Angus Johnson, Brian Smith and the staff of Shetland Museum; Suzanne Parsons of Lochcarron Library; Stephen Moss; Eileen Scott; Tara Lee-Platt of the RSPB; my son Angus Murray who pointed out *Hebridean Sharker* to me; Donald W Gillies, Donald Macleod, Iain Gillies, Murdo Morrison from South Dell; Keith, Sara, Emilie, Leslie, Nicola, Elwood, Patti who either accompanied me to Holy Isle or showed me the way; John Morrison of North Uist and Glasgow for his kindness; Arthur Cormack of Fèisean nan Gàidheal and Floraidh Forrest of Tobar an Dualchais, who were extremely valuable in terms of Gaelic song and folklore. (Arthur even took me north to Gairloch one evening for a Gaelic ceilidh where, among others, his daughter Eilidh was singing.) I am very lucky in both being bilingual and having contacts in all Scotland's island communities on whom I can draw.

I was also fortunate in those that came before me. Craig Mair's *A Star for Seamen* – published by John Murray in 1978 – first whetted my appetite for tales of lighthouses and lightkeepers when I encountered it over 30 years ago. My enthusiasm and interest for the topic have been sharpened by the numerous works I have read on this topic over the years since, including those mentioned in the bibliography. Many of these are wonderful reads and I would recommend them thoroughly. Some – like Bella Bathurst's work – are much more traditional histories than *For the Safety of All*, which is principally a work of narrative non-fiction. On a personal level, I would like to thank Michael Strachan – who gave me time and support during my visit to Kinnaird Head lighthouse – and John Love, whom I have known for many years. His work was especially valuable when I wrote the natural history section of this book. I was also fortunate in knowing the late Lawrence Tulloch. He and I had a long conversation about lighthouses in Lerwick Tesco's once. It was there that he made the remark that provides one of the chapter headings in this book – though I have to admit it was Davie Walker from South Uist and Glasgow who reminded me of what he said!

I would like to thank the inhabitants of Lochcarron for their help in this work. They provided a home from home for me while I wrote the first draft of this book. This is especially true of the large number with Ness connections whom I met during my stay in the village. *Tapadh leibh uile*. A special note of gratitude has to be in place for the Macleod and McMillan families, including Cathy, Carol, Flora, Joan and Euan. They were among those who provided tea, coffee and helped keep loneliness at bay. My gratitude to you all.

Yet there are people to whom a greater debt even than those mentioned above is owed. They include the staff of the Northern Lighthouse Board, especially Fiona Holmes, who was a marvellous contact throughout, and Peter Mackay, former NLB Chair.

At Historic Environment Scotland, thanks go to Alasdair Burns, who arranged the astonishing array of photographs found within its covers: and Christine Wilson, who was a wonderfully effective editor, continually reminding me of its purpose and providing these pages with an edge and energy they would have otherwise lacked. I am grateful for all their input and hard work. They impressed me throughout this long endeavour. Thanks also to their HES colleagues, including Philip Robertson, Simon Montgomery, Tom Parnell, Oliver Brookes, Ranald MacInnes, Elizabeth McCrone, Kevin Munro, Ruairidh Graham, Kristina Watson, Veronica Fraser, and Derek Smart and the photographic and digitising services.

Finally, there are two other individuals to whom I would like to give thanks. One is my wife Maggie, who has given me so much love and support over the years. (It is not easy, I am all too aware, to live with a writer.) The other is John McMillan, who gave me the use and shelter of his house while he was abroad in late 2019. This enabled me to write the work at greater speed than I could ever have done while at home. It also allowed me to travel to various locations – such as Edinburgh, Arbroath, Skye, Fraserburgh and Gairloch – in order to undertake research during the most difficult time of year to voyage back and forth from Shetland. For such kindness and support, I can only express my wonder. A former headteacher and excellent raconteur and company, John is a remarkable individual whom I have learned to love, value and admire in the more than two decades since we met.

Tapadh leibh uile.

Le beannachdan,

Donald S Murray

Index

The Northern Lighthouse Board

Northern Lighthouse Board

The Northern Lighthouse Board is the General Lighthouse Authority for Scotland and the Isle of Man. It has provided this vital safety service to mariners since its formation by an Act of Parliament in 1786. Originally tasked with the construction of just four lighthouses– Kinnaird Head, North Ronaldsay, Scalpay and Mull of Kintyre – it gained a reputation for engineering excellence as the number of lighthouses increased in and around the Scottish coast. This was largely down to the engineer Robert Stevenson and his descendants. For over 150 years they designed and built the majority of Scotland's lighthouses. They constructed wonders of engineering that have withstood the test of time and the elements. You only have to look at Robert Stevenson's Bell Rock Lighthouse, which has been continuously safeguarding ships and the lives of seafarers since 1811, to recognise the remarkable contribution made to our nation.

Today, the Northern Lighthouse Board operates and maintains a range of radio aids to navigation, over 200 lighthouses and around 170 buoys, as well as overseeing the aids to navigation provided by others, including ports, harbours, fish farms and the offshore oil and gas industry.

The headquarters are in the centre of Edinburgh on George Street, in a building occupied by NLB since 1832. The formal Georgian facade of the building belies the twenty-first century organisation that operates within, which, while taking great pride in its heritage, has technological innovation and modernity at its heart. The main Operating Base is in Oban with berthing for NLB's two vessels, aviation facilities, extensive workshops and resources for refurbishing buoys. Small teams of technicians who maintain the aids to navigation are based in Edinburgh and Oban as well as Inverness, Orkney and Shetland.

The work of NLB makes a significant contribution to the prevention of accidents and incidents around the coastline, safeguarding lives and property, and protecting the precious marine environment. By keeping sea lanes open and trade moving, the organisation directly benefits the economies of Scotland and the Isle of Man. It also aids economic development through investment in high quality training, by offering apprenticeship opportunities for young people and providing support to the fishing, aquaculture and tourism industries.

For more information on the Northern Lighthouse Board, please visit www.nlb.org.uk

Dubh Artach Lighthouse, Argyll & Bute A Listed
The *Pharos* moored near Dubh Artach. Built in 1872, this structure was put in place to prevent shipwrecks on the Torrin Rocks, allowing vessels to find safe anchorage in ports and harbours such as Oban and Colonsay.
Ian Cowe

Historic Environment Scotland

HISTORIC | ÀRAINNEACHD
ENVIRONMENT | EACHDRAIDHEIL
SCOTLAND | ALBA

From our towns and cities to our countryside and treacherous storm-swept coastlines, you are never far from a special site or place in Scotland. Shaped by people for over 10,000 years, our country is home to some of the most celebrated buildings and landscapes in the world.

One of Historic Environment Scotland's roles is to celebrate that legacy for future generations by giving legal recognition to sites and places which are an important part of our history. We call this designation. Listed buildings are the most well-known type of designation, but we are also responsible for designating scheduled monuments (archaeological sites and structures) and historic battlefields, as well as gardens and designed landscapes.

We believe these places are among Scotland's greatest assets. They chart our history and highlight our distinctiveness. They help to make Scotland a great place and allow us to understand who we are. Ranging from sites over 8,000 years old to buildings constructed in the 1990s, they cover many aspects of our lives – from how we lived and worked, fought

and worshipped, to how we spent our leisure time. This varied and exceptional heritage is witness to the vision and skill of our predecessors. Designation helps us to recognise their achievements and pass them on to future generations.

And our noble lighthouses are a part of this. Standing sentinel on our coasts it is easy to admire them as familiar yet striking landmarks, and just as easy to forget the incredible engineering skill of those who risked their lives to build them, making our seas a safer place. Built for a practical purpose, but with an enduring elegance, they are now much-loved and, in some strange way, romantic and enigmatic emblems of our coastlines.

Designating a site or place doesn't mean it has to stay the same forever. It simply means the history and special character of a place are considered when changes are being planned. Every year permission is given by planning authorities for thousands of listed buildings to be altered to help them meet new needs. We welcome applications asking us to assess sites and places for designation as well as your views about sites under consideration for designation. Together we can help to make sure that future generations will be able to enjoy our outstanding heritage.

Further information about designations can be found at www.historicenvironment.scot

Lismore Lighthouse, Argyll & Bute A Listed

Erected at the entrance to Loch Linnhe in the Firth of Lorne, this tower was built in 1833.

HES 008-000-012-800-R